THE
POWER
OF
PARTNERING

Vision, Commitment, and Action

Joanne Genova Sujansky, Ph.D.

Pfeiffer
& COMPANY

San Diego • Toronto • Amsterdam • Sydney

Pfeiffer & Company
8517 Production Avenue
San Diego, California 92121
619-578-5900 FAX: 619-578-2042

Editor:
Marian K. Prokop

Cover, Design, and Page Composition:
Kris Kircher

This book is printed on acid-free, recycled
stock that meets or exceeds the minimum GPO
and EPA specifications for recycled paper.

Dedication

To Charles Sujansky, my life partner,
and to our children,
Cara and Justin.

Preface

When executives, managers, supervisors, employees, and consultants work together toward a clear vision, they maximize their business. Conversely, when they do not work in this way, they hurt the business. Lack of direction, win-lose behaviors, lack of commitment, and poor planning always have negative effects on work output. When people work collaboratively toward clearly defined expectations, they are *partnering*. This book is about partnering, about people striving to solve organizational problems and to seek new opportunities. Partners respect, challenge, and empower one another as they work together to strengthen the business.

The Power of Partnering offers a strategic approach for maximizing the business by maximizing the human resources within an organization. It acknowledges people as the key to the organization's future. Partnering is based on the principles of collaboration and empowerment, but it is not limited to any one group or level of people. Rather, it is a description of effective behaviors and the tools and techniques that any person can use to increase the overall effectiveness and success of an organization. Although partnering embraces the collaborative approaches of team building and participative management, it is different. First, partnering is not limited to techniques that managers use with their staff members. Partnering puts a unique form on the collaborative approach, committing and empowering individuals and groups at all levels of an organization. Second, partnering behaviors are useful in both short- and long-term relationships and, third, partnering is useful in one-on-one and group interactions. The principle of partnering is "together we can solve problems and maximize opportunities." Therefore, the power of partnering is the power of joint problem solving and decision making *and* the focus on moving an organization forward creatively through opportunities.

This book is directed largely to managers in the work place, because they have primary responsibility for initiating partnerships. The techniques, however, are useful to those holding non-managerial positions, because they too are partners. This book is an aid for consultants, especially those involved in organizational change efforts. Many people have commented that the partnering behaviors have applications in their personal lives. I agree wholeheartedly, although I have not elaborated on that position in the book. I am committed to partnering as a way to create new and better products and services, as a way to make work challenging and meaningful, and as a way for the business to do its very best in the marketplace.

The Power of Partnering describes how to form, nurture, and manage partnerships between managers, employees, and consultants. It is concerned with providing techniques for developing effective partnerships, evaluating the progress of partnerships, and becoming a more effective organizational member.

Chapter I describes partnering and how organizations can benefit from it. Partnerships are based on vision, commitment, and action, as described in Chapter II. Partnerships create a climate in which people are recognized for their contributions, in which mistakes are seen as part of the creative process, in which each person understands the big picture and how he or she fits into it, and in which work force diversity is welcomed because each person's uniqueness is valued.

Chapters III through V illustrate operating models for developing various types of partnerships. They guide potential partners through the process of creating effective partnerships between managers, between managers and employees, and between managers and consultants. Practical suggestions and techniques for setting expectations, recognizing achievers and identifying needs are provided.

Chapter VI describes how to monitor results and how to overcome obstacles along the way. It addresses the time and practice necessary to employ partnering techniques, and it also contains a tool for evaluating partnering behaviors.

To obtain the greatest benefit from *The Power of Partnering,* read it completely for an overall view. Then return to the chapter that describes the partnership form you are interested in developing.

The "Taking Action" section at the end of each chapter provides a guide for applying these principles to a specific situation. The steps presented here are not strict prescriptions; rather, they are a systematic set of ideas and actions for guiding the creative process involved in effective human relationships.

In my work as a consultant, as a manager, and as a business owner, I have become most committed to partnering. Through extensive experience, I have witnessed transformations within organizations as a result of employing the power of partnering. I encourage you to practice the techniques described in these chapters. As you gain experience with them, they will become an enhancement to your existing knowledge and skills.

Joanne G. Sujansky, Ph.D.
June, 1991

Acknowledgments

The Power of Partnering was written with the help of many people and was possible because of the exciting and challenging experiences that I have had over the years with my employers, my clients, and my staff. Although it is impossible to acknowledge each person who helped me to write this book, I wish to mention a few of them because of their special contributions.

To Jennifer Craig and Anne Louise Conlon Feeny, for their editing work and content recommendations.

To Charles (Chuck) Sujansky, my husband, a senior human resources manager, for his guidance and support throughout the writing process.

To Dr. Jan Ferri-Reed, JGS, and Deborah Fairbanks, Training Consultant, the two primary contributors. Jan has worked with me since 1985 to develop these partnering concepts for our client companies. Deborah developed the book's format and helped me with the how-to techniques. Her work greatly enhanced the manuscript.

Thanks, partners!

Contents

Chapter IV
Partnering with Employees

47

A Manager's Role in a Partnership • The Employee's Role in a Partnership • Creating the Manager-Employee Partnership • Vision and Commitment • Action • Analysis: The B & E Manufacturing Company • Summary • Taking Action

Chapter V
Partnering with Consultants

81

The Role of a Consultant • How To Select an Appropriate Consultant • Building A Partnership—Vision and Commitment • Examples of Partnering Situations • Summary • Taking Action

Chapter VI
Monitoring Results &
Overcoming Obstacles

103

Creating a Vision of Partnering • Making Commitments • Putting Partnering into Action • Summary • Taking Action

Chapter

I

WHY PARTNER?

I am easily satisfied with the very best.

—Winston Churchill

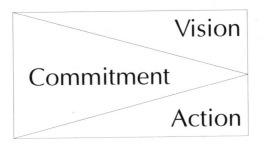

Today's competitive business environment dictates the need for organizations to develop effective ways to improve products and services and to increase profitability. When a product or service meets a need, when sales soar, when employee participation is encouraged and recognized, and when managers seize opportunities, partnering is at work. Successful corporate leaders, managers, and employees in today's business arena are discovering the power of partnering.

Simply put, partnering involves two or more individuals working collaboratively toward a desired outcome. Effective partnering is characterized by a collaborative mode of working together, resulting in win-win situations. Effective partners envision and create a flexible working environment in which authority is shared, each person is challenged to do his or her very best, and all are involved in the process of improving the product, the service, and the bottom line. Bonded in a partnership, people are challenged to solve problems and to seize opportunities. Partnering is dynamic and ever changing as it moves the organization forward.

Partners commit to working together toward desired results. Partnering calls for each person to show respect for the other, to put personal differences aside, and to focus on what the business needs from each of them. It is possible even for incompatible people to partner. Partners need not love one another; they simply must demonstrate respect for one another.

Sharing a vision and a commitment, partners are effective when they complement one another—sharing resources and opportunities for growth based on specific goals. Implementing a mutual plan of action, partners know and apply specific partnering behaviors that create winners.

Partnering is a new way of working together in business. Partnering integrates and systematically applies concepts of employee involvement, team building, and participative management—and provides an effective approach to navigating the challenges of today's organizational life.

The Purpose of Partnering

Establishing partnering relationships is critical to the effectiveness of an organization. Two major functions of partnering contribute to an organization's overall growth and success: solving problems and seizing opportunities. Future growth and strength are built on this foundation. To compete in a challenging external environment, an organization must first have a secure internal environment.

When problems are being solved, the company can move forward, learning from those problems and solutions. Successful problem solving provides an advantage not only in competing but also in forecasting or predicting other potential problems.

Healthy organizations are as involved in seizing opportunities as they are in solving problems. If partners are constantly looking over their shoulders at problems or fighting fires, they cannot be effective in scouting out new ways in which to expand the business, to streamline efforts, to change products, or to beat the competition. They must be encouraged by the corporation, by management, and by the partnership to look beyond themselves and beyond the present to where the company can go in the future.

Where Partnering Is Needed

Successful organizations develop and nurture partnering at all levels. Figure 1 shows the potential partnerships that managers can create within the organization, consisting of the following:

1. Managers and employees;
2. Managers and other managers;
3. Managers and internal consultants; and
4. Managers and external consultants.

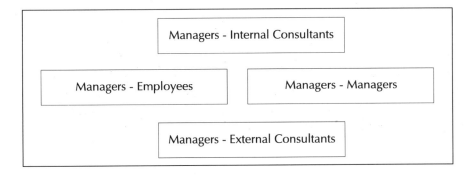

Figure 1. Partnerships Within the Organization

Partnering ultimately links individuals through open, two-way communication, thus enabling organizations to meet the challenges of the emerging business environment successfully.

How Partnering Enhances Organizations

What happens when partnerships are formed within an organization? Managers partnering with employees, managers partnering with consultants, and managers partnering with other managers all help to move corporations to positions of greater strength. Partnering creates a supportive organizational environment that benefits everyone. Such an environment ensures that all people, regardless of their levels in the organization, have the following experiences:

- Understanding how their work fits into the big picture and being challenged to make significant contributions;
- Believing in the company and in its desire to produce the best products or services;
- Feeling recognized for their talents, experience, and contributions;

- Knowing that making mistakes is part of the process of growing and innovating;
- Seeing that success is celebrated and that rewards come to those who earn them;
- Accepting work-force diversity as an advantage to the business; and
- Knowing that the quality of each employee's work life is important to the organization.

As an organization begins to partner, it develops a climate that recognizes, nurtures, and encourages the efforts of partnering. A partnering climate cultivates problem solvers and opportunity seekers. Partnering thrives when the organization's behavior supports the belief that people are its most valuable resource. Within this environment, people willingly seek partnering opportunities. Managers, employees, and consultants clearly understand that the gain effected by partnering is a gain for everyone. Successful partnerships foster the creation of other successful partnerships.

The chapters that follow describe how to create successful partnerships.

Analysis: The B & E Manufacturing Company

A medium-sized U.S. firm, referred to here as B & E Manufacturing, struggled with a classic problem: the rift between sales and production. Lee, the production manager said, "We cannot deliver what the salespeople are promising. They price jobs without considering the real cost of materials and labor. They promise delivery dates that hardly give us enough time to complete the specs. They should take off their suits, put on uniforms, and work this line for a while. Then they'd see the whole picture."

Terry, the sales manager, argued, "If production worked harder and smarter, they could deliver what we sell. They don't understand how tough it is to penetrate the market. We know our product is good, but we have competitors out there who can make the same product faster and cheaper. If it weren't for us, there wouldn't be a company."

The lack of partnering between Lee and Terry caused serious problems, evidenced by customers threatening to do business elsewhere. The challenge was to unite these departments, through their managers, in an effort to create a partnering environment and close communication gaps. "Partnering" sessions with an external consultant resulted in the managers realizing their interdependency, with a mutual need to take the following actions:

- To communicate clearly and often;
- To share information in a timely manner; and
- To watch for ways to improve the work done in both departments.

As a result, production workers were provided with customer feedback and specific information about competitors. This motivated them to strive for reduced costs and improved turnaround time. Salespeople were given specific material and labor costs as well as guidelines for determining production time. Salespeople asked a lot of questions of the production managers and the exchange led to an increased understanding of the challenges in production. The sales group got renewed faith in the quality of the product and committed themselves to sell that as a primary benefit to clients.

The two managers formed a a dynamic partnership in which both understood the value of moving together toward company goals as well as toward their own departmental goals. Through collaboration, they stabilized their client base and actually increased sales within one year.

Summary

Recognizing people as a company's most valuable resource unleashes people's creativity and acknowledges partnering as a primary catalyst to move the company forward. Building a climate that nurtures the growth of partnerships and rewards partnering behavior is a worthwhile effort. As partners become more participative, they begin to solve problems and to seize opportunities, resulting in companies that are more flexible. Partners seek to identify problems, to offer solutions, and to share ideas and resources. They are committed to a successful change process.

Companies that succeed at partnering are able to create models for themselves. They examine their successes to forecast where, when, and how to do business in the future. Dynamic businesses led by dynamic partners have a distinct advantage—they can compete and strive together toward a position of innovation and growth.

TAKING ACTION

Take a moment to respond to these questions in order to focus on the value of partnering for you.

1. Do you work in an environment in which authority is shared, in which each person is challenged to do his or her very best, and in which each person is involved in the process of improving the product, the service, and the bottom-line?

2. Do you currently challenge others to solve problems collaboratively and to seize opportunities?

3. Do you share a commitment with others to work together toward desired results in your group, department,
   or organization?

4. In what ways could partnering enhance your work
   environment?

Chapter

II

THE INGREDIENTS OF EFFECTIVE PARTNERSHIPS

Whatever you can do, or dream you can, begin it.
Boldness has genius, power, and magic in it.

—J.W. Goethe

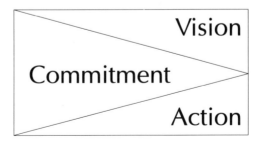

In 1887 a partnership began that lasted forty-nine years. Unlike others who saw no hope for the blind, deaf, mute child named Helen Keller, Annie Sullivan had a plan. Annie's first step was to convince Helen of her capabilities, one success at a time.

Soon the unmanageable, desperate child began to make slow but steady progress toward becoming a self-sufficient adult. First she learned to read and write in Braille. By the age of ten, Helen learned to speak; by age sixteen she entered a preparatory school. The partnership between Helen Keller and Annie Sullivan flourished as Helen went on to become a famous author and lecturer. Guided by a dream, two people worked together to achieve what appeared to be impossible.

Like Keller and Sullivan, partners strive toward dreams one step at a time. They compare their current situations to their visions of the future. They proceed through a series of well-planned steps that ensure that their goals are met and that their vision becomes a reality.

It is natural for some partnering efforts to be short term, such as in the case of a task force formed to create a positive discipline system. Other partnering efforts are long term, like the one formed between a supervisor and a staff member. Regardless of the life span of the partnering relationship, partners work on problems and opportunities to ensure quality outcomes. They abandon ineffective practices and keep goals in sight.

The Ingredients of Effective Partnerships

Whether change occurs through solving problems or through seizing opportunities, partners can be only as successful in these activities as they are in their partnerships. Effective partnerships have the following three main ingredients:

1. A *vision* of what the partners want to accomplish and how they will use partnering to get there;
2. A *commitment* to specific goals as well as to the partnership; and
3. A plan of *action* to accomplish these goals, including responsibilities, project resources, and deadlines.

Vision

Vision is a clear picture of what can be. It creates the focus, the hope, and the dream of what a partnership can accomplish. Vision motivates and requires partners to act. It fosters positive, creative, and synergistic thinking.

Ideally, vision is created by all partners and translated into a direction or purpose. Sometimes individuals come into the partnership with vision and direction already identified, dictated by corporate need. The partnership need not suffer as long as all partners understand the vision and are included in the action-planning process.

The vision of the partners also includes an image of working together successfully. Envisioning the use of partnering behaviors, partners anticipate their success.

Commitment

Commitment is an internal decision that a person makes when he or she says, "I see the need for this change, I believe in it, and I will make it work." A partner sees that the partnership itself offers a way to make the vision a reality. This person commits to the changes to be made and to his or her part in the partnership. Of course commitment comes easily in an environment in which people have seen and tasted success.

Commitment and vision are double threads, overlapping and reinforcing each other. Individuals who are committed to success easily envision success when forming a partnership. When forming a partnership and envisioning its success, individuals become committed through their unified energy.

Commitment can be seen in the case of a staff member who, faced with a production problem, stays after normal working hours to solve the problem. This person believes in the business and has a very clear picture of what that commitment can and will mean to him or her. This person demonstrates the spirit of "whatever it takes to get the job done." That commitment is supported by the fact that the person knows what to do, how to do it, and when the work should be completed.

The best way for management to gain commitment from others is to model it, to give positive reinforcement to those who demonstrate it, and to publicize partnering successes.

Action

Partnering requires creating a *vision* of what will be, making a *commitment* to the end results and to partnering as a beneficial managerial approach, and putting the knowledge and techniques of partnering into *action*. An action plan describes the specifics of who does what, when, and how. Partners take responsibility for setting objectives and for determining timetables for the completion of tasks. Although partners do not always share the load equally, each should carry his or her own weight. Partners must understand the importance of each person's contribution to the partnership and the consequences of not meeting these responsibilities. When these responsibilities are not met, the partnership deteriorates into a lose-lose situation.

Successful Partnering Behaviors

Any partnership with clear vision, strong commitment, and a plan of action can make a positive impact on a business. While vision, commitment, and action form the basis for partnering, specific behaviors ensure the success of the effort. The ten behaviors for successful partnering (Figure 2) are as follows:

1. **Identify the desired results.** Successful partners determine the expected outcomes and put them in writing. The expected outcomes should be specific and challenging, yet attainable. Because the outcomes determine the direction of the partnering effort, the written plan should include whatever is required to move the partnership forward. All partners must be focused in the same direction with their efforts supporting one another.

2. **Agree to make a difference.** Partners commit to the change effort with a sincere desire to make a difference. They partner to rid the company of an existing problem or to create new opportunities. They strive to improve the work environment and to better the organization's competitive position.

3. **Clarify roles**, especially those that may put individuals in roles that differ from their real jobs.

4. **Assess needs**. A willingness to identify mutual needs for information, skills, resources, and authority (along with a willingness to share them) builds trust, empowers partners, and opens the organization to growth and change.

5. **Recognize achievements.** This involves acknowledging success in terms of the desired results and the partnership itself.

6. **Make ongoing corrections.** Effective partners develop a relationship that allows for mistakes and encourages learning from them. People who have never failed may not have been trying hard enough. Partners learn from one another's errors so they can move ahead more effectively. They deal with what went wrong so that they can avoid similar mistakes in the future.

7. **Be willing to take risks,** to improve products or services, to increase productivity, and to maximize people and technology for the future. Partners acknowledge, understand, and share in

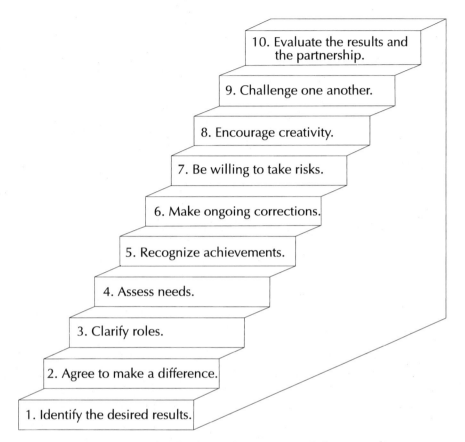

Figure 2. Ten Behaviors for Successful Partnering

risk taking for the organization and for themselves, thereby committing to the changes.

8. **Encourage creativity.** Partners are open to ideas and alternative ways of looking at problems, stimulating one another to find novel solutions and to explore possibilities.

9. **Challenge one another** by thinking of ways to make work more productive and interesting. When partners collaborate, they make one another's contributions count and give credit where it is due.

10. **Evaluate the results and the partnership.** Partners monitor the effectiveness of the relationship and the overall results from the partnership.

The tools and techniques described in the following chapters help partners to learn successful partnering behaviors. Envisioning and committing to success, combined with using partnering behaviors within a specific plan of action, enables partners to make the changes needed to improve and to expand their organizations.

Analysis: The B & E Manufacturing Company

The following situations at B & E Manufacturing illustrate the importance of forming partnerships.

> Ken, vice president of marketing, served on a task force to develop a hiring manual for managers. In this role, he did not direct the project's outcome or assign work as he might do in his role as vice president of marketing. Instead, Ken's talents and experiences were used to help another department to develop a product for all managers to use. When they formed this partnership, the task force members clarified their roles, especially those that put individuals in roles different from their real jobs. As long as partnering roles are comfortable and meaningful, partners will usually contribute appropriately and partnering expectations can be met.
>
> John, Marge, and George, the owners of B & E, lacked clear direction. Two of the three owners wanted to expand the business nationwide and be freed of any daily operations responsibilities. The third owner, however, preferred to stay with the single location in which the business was prospering. He was sure that expansion was too risky. In this situation, the owners' behaviors were not partnering behaviors. Not only were they in turmoil over their goals, but they also

confused their employees. As a result of negotiation, the owner who wanted one location sold his stock to the other two and established a similar but noncompetitive business. As the partners moved toward identifying the desired results of their efforts, they became focused in the same direction with their efforts supporting one another. When partners are not headed in the same direction and are not supporting one another's efforts, the partnership is headed for disaster.

Dale, the finance manager, and Chris, the client-service manager, were constantly at odds. They fought over every issue related to their departments. Dale fought for cost cuts while Chris fought for budget increases to extend services and to create new programs. In the midst of a budget battle, Chris proposed a revenue-generating new venture. Dale, usually unhappy with Chris's plans for new ventures, supported Chris's request for the funds needed to get started. They experienced the value of working together toward a common goal, discovered a new business opportunity, and generated increased revenues. By agreeing to make a difference, partnering served the best interests of the organization, of the two departments, and of Dale and Chris themselves.

Several design engineers, all of whom reported to the same manager, were frustrated by lack of role clarity. In an effort to determine priorities and expected outcomes, they began to develop goals and to submit them to their manager for approval. They made partnering successful for themselves and moved the department ahead in spite of the manager's lack of focus and direction. The situation might have been better if they had partnered with their manager; however, partnering with one another allowed them to clarify roles, to set priorities, to determine expected outcomes, and to make an organizational impact.

In an administrative department, a group of disgruntled employees struggled with their supervisors because they felt uninformed, out of touch, and slaves to outdated practices. Further examination by the new chief executive officer (CEO) revealed that employees were often left in the dark by supervisors who did not share information. New priorities included changing old habits, updating procedures and equipment, and establishing new vehicles of communication. The CEO wisely partnered with the group to assess needs for sharing information, skills, resources, and authority, thus modeling appropriate behavior. In three years, the CEO built an organization in which sharing of information, resources, and authority was the rule rather than the exception. A willingness to share these resources builds trust, empowers employees, and opens the organization to growth and change. These changes strengthened the company by empowering employees and managers to learn from and trust one another.

The managers of the public-relations department decided to develop and to offer a new, innovative service. They invested time and money developing and marketing it but never made a profit. The venture was a mistake, but they learned where they went wrong: they veered away from their original business focus. By making ongoing corrections, they became clearer about their mission and successfully expanded the existing services. In a sense, they created the future in part from what failure taught them.

The training manager at B & E realized that the department lacked prepackaged material that other divisions could use in place of customized training. The manager's new strategy was twofold: (1) to invest in the development of multimedia modules that could be custom fit for other groups, and (2) to form collaborative relationships with firms specializing in off-the-shelf training. The manager's willingness to take risks to improve products and services resulted in increased numbers of well-trained employees.

Karen, a new line worker, realized that it took her twice as long to stop production and check the containers she had made as it did to check all of her work at the end of her shift. Concerned about the time loss, Karen brought the problem to her supervisor, who asked for Karen's ideas about improving the situation. Karen suggested that while one employee was making containers, another could check their quality and pick up batches of new materials. The results of following Karen's suggestions were very favorable: the work continued to flow; each employee processed and verified, avoiding delays; the new procedure reduced process time; and production and quality increased. Having saved the company thousands of dollars, Karen was acknowledged through the employee-recognition program for her efforts.

Throughout the organization, partners monitored results against their action plans and milestone dates. Using evaluation tools, they assessed their partnering behaviors. Using the data from their evaluations, they challenged one another to address areas of poor performance creatively; they recognized successes; and they continued to improve by their willingness to assess needs, take risks, and make ongoing assessments and corrections.

Summary

Partners who share a vision are committed to that vision and understand their responsibilities clearly. Driven by a vision, partners brainstorm and listen to others' ideas, evaluating the pitfalls without closing the doors to creativity.

Partners seek collaboration and work to reach goals determined by the shared vision. Partners challenge one another, share information, learn from their mistakes, take risks, and move forward. Successful partnering creates an organization that prospers through the combined resources and talents of its members. Figure 3 illustrates a model statement of partnering.

A STATEMENT OF PARTNERING

We understand how our work fits into the big picture, and we are challenged to make significant contributions.

We believe in the company and in its desire to produce the best products or services.

We feel recognized for our talents, experience, and contributions.

We are willing to take risks to improve our products and services.

We know that making mistakes is part of the process of growing and innovating.

We find that success is celebrated and that rewards come to those who earn them.

We are committed to making a difference.

We accept work-force diversity as an advantage to the business.

We agree to challenge one another in the spirit of growth and improvement.

We know that the quality of each employee's work life is important to the organization.

Figure 3. Sample Statement of Partnering

TAKING ACTION

Check those statements that describe your relationships with others in your organization:

- ☐ We have a clear vision of what we want to accomplish.
- ☐ We understand how our work fits into the big picture.
- ☐ We see the benefits of collaborating in a unified direction.
- ☐ We share a commitment to our goals.
- ☐ We believe in the company and in its desire to produce the best products or services.
- ☐ We believe in making a difference in the marketplace.
- ☐ We have a plan of action.
- ☐ We have clearly defined roles and responsibilities.
- ☐ We assess our needs for information, skills, resources, and decision making.
- ☐ We share information in a timely manner.
- ☐ We seek creative ways to improve the work of our department/group.
- ☐ We give and receive recognition for our talents, experience, and contributions.
- ☐ We demonstrate the attitude that making mistakes is part of the process of growing and innovating.
- ☐ We ensure that success is celebrated.
- ☐ We accept work-force diversity as an advantage to the business.
- ☐ We believe that the quality of each employee's work life is important to the organization.

Chapter

III

PARTNERING WITH OTHER MANAGERS

Great things are not done by impulse,
but by a series of small things brought together.

—Vincent Van Gogh

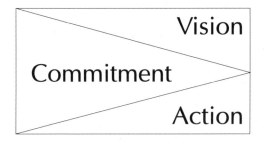

Partnering managers envision and commit to success. They continually assess opportunities to expand business operations or to solve problems. They continually seek out employees, other managers, and consultants with whom to form partnerships. They know that when they find others who are equally committed to making a difference in the organization, they can establish win-win relationships.

Partnering managers explore what could be gained from a partnership and weigh options carefully before deciding whether or not the partnership can work. Given a commitment, they share skills, interests, knowledge, and resources to develop new approaches, alternative solutions, and more realistic decisions for corporate change.

What follows is a step-by-step procedure for successful partnering. This chapter applies the procedure to the manager-to-manager partnership. The next chapter applies the procedure to manager-employee relationships.

Getting Ready

A partnering manager may consider partnering with another manager. For example, a manager of finance may choose to collaborate with a human resources manager to solve problems or to initiate changes within the organization. A partnership may be appropriate for working together on an improved benefits package or for working collaboratively to investigate a new profit-sharing plan.

To determine whether or not to develop a partnership, a partnering manager asks:

- Do I prefer to work in a win-win situation?
- Do I perceive more benefits than problems when I ask others for their ideas, suggestions, and opinions?

- Do I want all partners to define expected results together?
- What will be gained by partnering with another manager?
- Am I willing to challenge and be challenged by the other party?
- Am I willing to invest time to establish the partnership?
- Am I willing to explore new and different solutions to problems?
- Am I willing to seek and to pursue opportunities that will benefit both departments and the organization?
- Am I willing to invest time and resources to evaluate any changes that are made?

Vision and Commitment

Partnering managers believe in the value of shared vision and clear direction. They set mutual goals collectively and pursue them actively. A partnering manager develops a clear, strategic direction and gains commitment with another manager by taking the following steps:

1. Clarify the problem or opportunity;
2. Agree to make a difference, which sets the tone for a high-achieving partnership; and
3. Envision the success of the partnership by employing partnering behaviors throughout the relationship.

Successful partners know what exists currently and are clear about what they desire. They also anticipate changes that will occur. Because anticipating changes requires a shared vision, partners spend whatever time is needed to create that shared vision.

Action

Once partners make a partnering commitment, they follow a logical process to reach their goals. They provide and share resources; they nourish idea development; they take pride in achieving expected results; and they recognize their accomplishments. Planning, diagnosing, making decisions, implementing, and evaluating are the basic phases in the partnering process.

Planning

Whether the partnering is to be short- or long-term, the partners must define what they want to accomplish. During this planning phase, partners address the following tasks:

Set goals. Effective partners determine what they want to achieve. They set goals that are specific, measurable, realistic, and challenging.

Identify each partner's role. Effective partners clarify their roles and specific responsibilities.

Determine how to analyze a situation or diagnose a problem. Effective partners decide how they will study an existing problem or investigate possibilities for pursuing an opportunity. They consider methodologies; they explore costs, timing, and feasibility; and they decide who will conduct the diagnosis and why.

Establish time lines. Effective partners establish realistic time lines. They determine the desired date of implementation and work back from there to set other task-completion dates.

Determine resources needed. Effective partners determine what resources they will need in order to accomplish their goals. They estimate the number of people needed and calculate costs. These costs can include fees and out-of-pocket expenses for those hired from outside the organization, as well as expenses for internal workers if travel and frequent meetings are required. Other known costs, such as those for the diagnosis phase or costs for securing data, should be included as well.

Decide on an evaluation process. Effective partners determine ongoing and final evaluation processes and decide on a feedback system that they will use as they pursue their goals. To do so, they establish checkpoints and processes for evaluating their progress. As part of this phase, partners also establish methods for assessing the effects of the changes they achieve and for evaluating their partnering process. Evaluation of the partnering relationship is accomplished with feedback sessions, using questions like those that appear later in this chapter.

Document the agreement. If partners work solely from a verbal contract, they risk confusion about responsibilities and expected results. Each partner needs a clear understanding of how and when decisions are to be made. By outlining specific timetables, results, and responsibilities, the partners avoid misunderstandings. The contract records the partners' commitments to one another. The format can vary, but the agreement, contract, or work plan should be agreed on by all and put in writing. This document outlines the path to achieve success and avoid misunderstandings. Figure 4 illustrates a format that summarizes the key steps in the planning phase.

Completing the planning phase is critical to the success of the project and of the partnering relationship. Projects fail when partners move from identifying the problem or opportunity to diagnosing it, skipping the steps in between or defining them too loosely. Using this sample format to review projects that failed in the past can help to determine where and how they could have been saved.

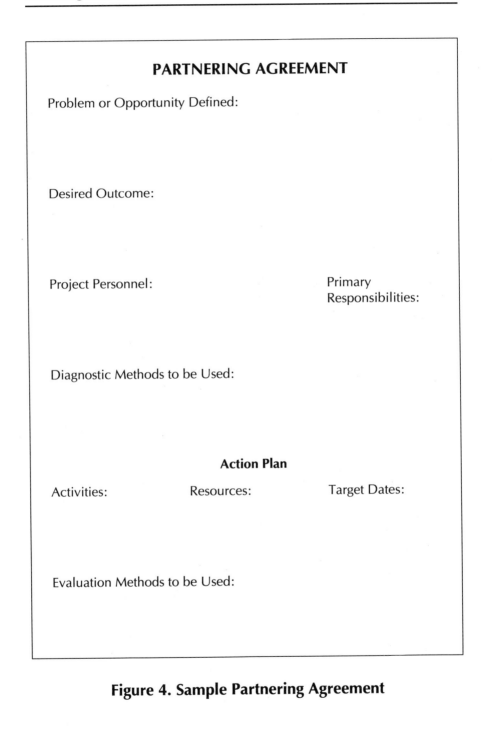

Figure 4. Sample Partnering Agreement

Diagnosing Problems and Opportunities

This phase requires data collection or fact finding as well as analysis. When solving a problem, effective partners may find that some facts revealed in the diagnosis phase are causes while others are symptoms. Analyzing data determines their real causes. When developing an opportunity, effective partners examine the driving forces or conditions that support the opportunity. They also determine restraining forces or those conditions that could hinder seizing the opportunity.

Various diagnostic techniques aid in collecting the necessary data. The responsibility for diagnosis is shared equally in most partnerships. However, in some partnerships one partner may have more responsibility than the others. This might occur if one partner is more skilled in diagnostic techniques, if he or she has data already available, or if he or she is more objective than the others involved.

It is important to do the diagnosis according to the decisions that were made in the planning phase. The results of the diagnosis and the techniques used to gather data then are shared with the other partners to ensure objectivity and appropriateness of techniques. This keeps the others informed and helps them learn collection and analysis techniques.

The following section, although not all inclusive, presents the advantages and disadvantages of four diagnostic techniques that are commonly used in the partnering process:

Direct observation. This diagnostic technique is done within the work setting. Direct observation is more accurate if the observer is not visible or if the person who is observing appears to be nonthreatening. Watching behavior firsthand allows a partner to gather accurate data in the "real" environment. The observer may record all occurrences and behaviors chronologically as they happen or may list all behaviors that focus on one aspect of the problem or opportunity. Data then are categorized and analyzed as needed. Partners need to keep in mind that direct observation may cause the people who are being observed to act or behave unnaturally, which can skew the data. However, repeated observations may help to reduce this possibility. Partners also need to be careful that their personal biases do not interfere with watching and recording events objectively. Partners can reduce this tendency by recording the data in behavioral terms and by refraining from stating opinions. Another caution about direct observation is that it is time consuming; therefore time lines must be set accordingly.

Questionnaires and surveys. Although time consuming to design, written documents can obtain data from a large group of people relatively quickly. Survey responses also may be more candid because anonymity is provided. Despite these advantages, written tools also have limitations. For example, partners may not know the reasons behind a respondent's choices. In addition, if a respondent does not understand what is being asked, there is no way for partners to explain.

Interviewing. Partners can question those involved in the partnering effort to determine their perceptions of the problem or opportunity, their feelings, and their attitudes. Interviews allow the partners to probe responses and observe nonverbal behaviors. Interviewing, however, requires an objective and skilled interviewer and eliminates anonymity for the person being interviewed.

Existing data. Partners can review data that are readily available. Use of existing written data lessens the danger of contrived responses or behaviors that might occur when using other diagnostic tools. Partners should recognize that existing data could be limiting if used alone. Partners can weigh the benefits of reviewing existing data against the time required to secure the information through other means.

Making Decisions

Armed with objective data, partners proceed to the decision phase, in which they begin to make decisions about what should happen in order to achieve the desired end results.

Partners structure and report the recommended decisions according to the contract created in the planning phase. The partner making the recommendations may be a marketing professional suggesting a marketing plan for a new product to the marketing vice president. Or the partner may be the internal or external training specialist proposing a training plan to a line manager who has asked for help because of productivity problems.

Regardless of the problem or opportunity, partners are wise to consider more than one solution or recommendation. Diagnosis frequently leads to a set of recommendations rather than a single suggested course of action. Effective partners explore options by weighing the pros and cons of each.

With a clear definition of the goals of the partnership, partners then make decisions while keeping in mind the company's available resources and potential risks and/or gains for the company or partners involved. In order to make decisions, partners follow these steps:

1. Summarize the information gathered in the diagnosis phase.
2. List all recommended options, including the pros and cons of each.
3. Select the option to present for consideration.
4. Provide documentation for all options, including an analysis of risks versus gains.
5. Consider what will need to be done to implement each option, because this may be a deciding factor in choosing it.
6. Conduct these steps in a meeting of all partners, and use a written document as a resource during and after the meeting.

The possible options to be considered are described as specifically and as realistically as possible, considering money, time, and resources. A sample format for written presentation of the final set of options is shown in Figure 5.

Given a set of decisions, partners may be ready to move into the implementation phase or they may need time to digest the

Option	Support Data	Risk	Gain	Imple- mentation Strategy
#1				
#2				
#3				
#4				

Figure 5. Sample Format for Written Options

options and discuss them further. They may even want to take the recommendations to a higher level for review and/or approval. If the partners represent a task force assigned to action, they can move into the implementation phase, approaching their destination with commitment.

Implementing Plans

Entering the implementation phase, partners market a new idea or product or change a course of action. The implementation phase begins with a very detailed plan of the tasks, specific people required, and resources to be involved. The implementation phase requires the partners to do the following:

Sell the new ideas to those who will be affected by the changes, especially those who have not been involved up to this point. For example, if the marketing plan for a new product is accepted by the marketing boss and is deemed "doable" by the senior team, it is time to share the plan with everyone who will be involved in the work.

Detail a specific plan for all involved, describing what is to be done, by whom, and when. For example, a line manager who has recommended a major training effort for his or her staff needs to decide what the training will include, how to ensure skill transfer to the job, what the training schedule will be, and who will do it.

Determine checkpoints to ensure that the partnering relationship is on course. For example, in one hotel chain's comprehensive change effort, partners from various locations met quarterly to assess how the plan was working and how their relationships were enhancing or impeding it.

Establish evaluation methods to be used throughout the change effort to ensure that tasks are successful. For example, if focus groups are to look at products that might be offered by a professional society, they will need to determine what criteria will be used to evaluate whether or not they are on track.

Establish the final evaluation process. For instance, in the previous training example, the "final" evaluation would involve measuring productivity three to six months after training.

Move at an appropriate rate. A rate that is appropriate for the change effort means looking not just at time and money, but also at people's abilities to accept the changes. Partners need to move carefully, ensuring understanding and securing "buy in."

As the implementation phase progresses, partners and others in the organization will begin to see the results and benefits of partnering. In the next phase, partners evaluate both the success of the effort and the quality of the partnership.

Evaluating Results

Effective partners evaluate their results after completing the other phases in the process. An integral part of any partnering evaluation includes examining the methods used and the results achieved.

During evaluation, partners examine the checkpoints established during the planning phase. At these checkpoints, each partner verifies the effectiveness of the relationship and the contributions each is making. Partners also look at results and decide whether or not they are truly achieving the changes that they originally wanted. If they have become sidetracked or if their direction is unclear, they can immediately make adjustments, thereby averting failure and saving time and resources.

When partners have clear, concise goals, specific roles, and definite time lines, evaluation is not difficult. Difficulty comes as a result of confused goals, undefined roles, and unclear or unstated deadlines. Like a road map, the partnership plan has clear signposts and is easy to understand. Effective partners know where they need to be at the beginning, the midpoint, and the end of the journey. They set times to evaluate both the partnership relationship and the accomplishments.

To evaluate the partnership itself partners ask the following questions:

1. What do we feel contributes to our working well together?
2. What hinders our working relationship?
3. What might we do differently in the future?
4. Are we upholding our commitments to one another?

When partners evaluate the relationship among themselves, they reinforce what is going well and correct what is not going well. They assess whether the relationship enhances or detracts from the goal. The future of the existing partnership—as well as that of further partnering efforts—depends on honest evaluation.

To evaluate the accomplishments, partners ask the following questions:

1. What are the evidences of success?
2. Are we on schedule? If not, why not?
3. Are we working within our allotted resources? If not, why not?

4. Have we been working smart, using the best methods possible? If not, how can we improve? What specific plan can we make to do so?

The advantage of evaluating outcomes periodically is that partners can identify any difficulty early on and can redirect their efforts. This not only saves time and money but also builds credibility for the partners. Evaluating helps partners to track their successes and provides vital information to the company about where they have been, where they are going, and if they are traveling at the proper speed.

Analysis: The B & E Manufacturing Company— Partnerships Between Managers

In the following example, partners used the operating model to effect a successful change.

A senior manager decided to develop a performance-management system and asked other managers within the firm to meet to discuss their needs. The group mapped a commitment and plan for fulfilling the organization's needs that included the following:

1. Suggestions for creating a performance-management system;
2. Project outlines with appropriate approaches and resources;
3. Internal and external staffing requirements; and
4. Costs for the project.

The group submitted the proposal to the chief executive officer (CEO) and found that the proposed costs exceeded the budget that had been allocated. Demonstrating partnership skills, the group submitted a second proposal showing how a greater portion of the work could be done internally, which reduced the cost. Group members listed the risks they saw—primarily overloading internal people, which could make the job tougher for them. In this way, all of the components necessary for making the project work were still intact. The group members did not compromise the suggested approach by accommodating a potential partner's needs; rather, they set the stage for building a strong partnership.

After accepting the proposal, the managers partnered with the external consultant, the CEO, and upper management to clarify needs. In the *planning phase,* they clarified roles and responsibilities for each stage. They discovered that the senior staff desired a more participatory culture. They brainstormed ways to involve employees actively in the process. The partners also identified roles and outlined a tentative time frame for the project.

For *diagnosis,* they chose interviewing and observation techniques, agreeing to maintain the confidentiality of individual sources. The partners designed a process for assessing the results of the project. Then the CEO, together with the partners, shared the goals of the project with all of the organization's employees. They described methods to be used in the diagnosis and projected time frames for each stage.

During the diagnostic phase, a designated group member gathered information by interviewing upper-level managers and other employees, some individually and others in groups. Then the group reviewed previously established policies, past attempts at conducting performance appraisals, and content from previous management-training programs.

The partners established trust and credibility, defusing the employees' concern about using outside help to develop the performance plans. They visited each location and observed employees performing their jobs. During these observations, they discovered more serious problems than they had anticipated. They immediately shared their concerns with management and discussed how to approach them. They clarified the parameters of the project and received commitment from top management to address those additional issues in the near future.

The partners presented written options for *decision making* to the CEO. The group had identified eleven major problem areas, most of which they believed could be taken care of by developing the following structures:

- A policies and procedures manual;
- Current position descriptions;
- A performance-planning system; and
- A means for performance feedback and evaluation.

Because the management staff was interested in a more participatory culture, the group also recommended varying levels of employee involvement throughout the process. Because of budget constraints, only the last two recommendations seemed possible. Management, however, decided to accept all four recommendations and to secure the money needed for implementing the first two recommendations. The problems that could not be resolved by the four recommendations were noted and acknowledged. The commitment to attend to them at a later date was announced to the employees.

The *implementation* plan described carefully planned employee-involvement activities. The initial phase involved developing the policy and procedures manual; the next phase involved writing the position descriptions; and the last phase involved designing performance planning, feedback, and evaluation. The work plan spanned a two-year period.

During the first implementation stage, the overload on the internal project manager became obvious. Deadlines were extended twice, which did not cause any serious concerns, but which did help to reduce the internal project manager's load. Additional work was also reassigned to the outside developers.

Clearly the time spent building the partnership in the planning phase secured a successful partnering process. *Evaluations,* which were done continuously as the project unfolded, also kept the partnership alive and well.

Throughout the two-year project, constant attention was given to the partners' roles, responsibilities, and deadlines. Results were evaluated as each phase was completed. Employees and managers evaluated the policies and procedures manual on its effectiveness as well as on its ease of use.

The partnerships between employees and managers and between managers also were evaluated. At one session, employees expressed concern that they were not as involved in decision making as they would like to be. During a discussion among the partners, the project manager suggested taking a more visible role in collaborating with the staff. Because employees were becoming increasingly participative—a primary goal of the intervention—it was important that they saw the shared authority of the internal people. Employees were involved at every step, from the development of the policies and procedures manual to the implementation of a performance planning, feedback, and evaluation system. As a result, a more participatory culture evolved and the partnership succeeded. Long-term evaluation systems were put in place to ensure that the new culture and the new tools developed continued to serve managers and employees.

Summary

The partnership model outlines steps to take in developing a partnership agreement to diagnose and to solve an existing problem or to research and to seize a new opportunity. Partners use insight to search for others who are well-matched, who have a vested interest in the goal, and who are willing to work mutually and collaboratively. The partners are systematic in their approach and specific about what they want to achieve whether they look to partner with other managers, employees, or consultants.

Armed with good data, partners consider alternate courses of action. They then develop a step-by-step plan, continually evaluating the results and the relationship.

This operating model offers guidance to both would-be and existing partners who form short- or long-term relationships. As they move through the model, solving problems or pursuing opportunities, they recognize that results are dependent on a collaborative, win-win, partnership effort. The partnership and all involved with it are, therefore, empowered to move the organization forward.

The following checklist is designed to provide guidance in developing partnerships.

1. ASSESS READINESS

- ☐ Do I prefer to work in a win-win situation?
- ☐ Do I perceive more benefits than problems when I ask others for their ideas, suggestions, and opinions?
- ☐ Do I want all partners to define expected results together?
- ☐ What will be gained by partnering with the other manager?
- ☐ Am I willing to challenge and be challenged by the other party?
- ☐ Am I willing to invest the time to establish the partnership?
- ☐ Am I willing to explore new and different solutions to problems?
- ☐ Am I willing to seek and pursue opportunities that will benefit both departments and the organization?
- ☐ Am I willing to invest the time and resources to evaluate any changes that we make?

2. VISION AND COMMITMENT—PROPOSE PARTNERSHIP

- ☐ Clarify the existence of a problem or opportunity.
- ☐ Identify the skills, information, or resources necessary to solve the problem or pursue the opportunity.
- ☐ Consider who might be the most likely choice for a partner.
- ☐ Contact the individual to discuss his or her perception of the problem or opportunity.
- ☐ Assess the other party's interest in working on the problem or opportunity.

☐ Consider the other person's style and how effectively you can work together.

☐ Discuss the problem or opportunity in detail to make certain the other party understands and has valuable insights for achieving final outcome.

☐ Express interest in forming a partnership.

3. TAKE ACTION

☐ **Planning**

    ☐ Clarify the problem or opportunity together.

    ☐ Set goals.

    ☐ Identify each partner's role.

    ☐ Determine the methods to be used to analyze a situation or diagnose a problem.

    ☐ Establish time lines.

    ☐ Determine resources needed.

    ☐ Decide on the evaluation process.

    ☐ Document the agreement.

☐ **Diagnosing Problems and Opportunities**

    ☐ Determine who will perform the diagnosis.

    ☐ Select the appropriate diagnostic techniques from the following list:

        ☐ Direct observation

        ☐ Questionnaires and surveys

        ☐ Interviewing

        ☐ Existing data

    ☐ Collect data.

    ☐ Analyze the data to determine real causes, including the following:

        ☐ Examining driving forces/conditions that support the opportunity.

    ☐ Determining restraining forces/conditions that could hinder seizing the opportunity.

☐ Making Decisions

    ☐ Summarize information gathered in the diagnosis phase.

    ☐ List all possible recommendations, including the pros and cons of each.

    ☐ Select recommendations to present for consideration.

    ☐ Provide substantiation for all recommendations, including an analysis of risks versus gains.

    ☐ Consider what will need to be done to implement each recommendation.

    ☐ Conduct these steps in a meeting of all partners, and use a written document as a resource during and after the meeting.

☐ Implementing Plans

    ☐ Sell the new ideas to those who will be affected by the changes, especially those not involved to this point.

    ☐ Detail a specific plan for all involved, describing what is to be done, by whom, and when.

    ☐ Determine checkpoints to ensure that the partnering relationship is on course.

    ☐ Establish evaluation methods to be used throughout the change effort to ensure that tasks are successful.

    ☐ Establish the final evaluation process.

    ☐ Move at a rate that is appropriate for the change effort.

☐ Evaluating Results

    ☐ Examine checkpoints established during the planning phase.

- ☐ Review results and decide if they are truly achieving the change that the partners had originally wanted; ask the following questions:
    - ☐ What are the evidences of success?
    - ☐ Are we on schedule? If not, why?
    - ☐ Are we working within our allotted resources? If not, why?
    - ☐ Have we been working smart, using the best methods possible?
    - ☐ If not, how can we improve?
    - ☐ What is the specific plan to do so?
- ☐ Evaluate the partnership, using the following questions:
    - ☐ What do we feel contributes to our working well together?
    - ☐ Is anything hindering our working relationship?
    - ☐ What might we do differently in the future?
    - ☐ Are we upholding the commitments we made to one another?
- ☐ Make any necessary adjustments.

Note: Further information on evaluating partnerships is provided in Chapter VI.

Chapter

IV

PARTNERING
WITH EMPLOYEES

---

*"A leader may chart the way... [but] many leaders
and many peoples must do the building."*

—Eleanor Roosevelt

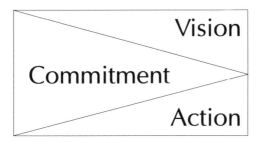

Recruit good talent, show them how to do it, let them know what they did right, have a game plan, encourage them, correct them, celebrate with them, feel the pain with them, push them hard, know their limits. This may sound like advice from a head coach to an assistant coach, but it is advice that any manager or supervisor should heed as well.

The following comments came from an employee who had been coached by his manager:

> During my interview, I remember thinking, "This woman really knows what she wants and what she wants the person in this job to do." It was a challenging interview. She wanted to know what impact I had made in my previous position. She was curious about my talents and whether I took initiative and creative approaches to the job. I left the interview hoping I would be selected; three weeks later I was on the job.
>
> I guess the term "empowered" describes how I feel. My boss speaks of "us," "our goals," "our direction," "our strategy." We have a lot to do, but we're doing it as a team. The atmosphere she strives for motivates me. She commonly describes us (her staff) as partners and expects that I'll work in a partnering way with my colleagues and staff, too.
>
> I feel informed in this job—something I've never felt before. She goes to bat for me when I need her; she's a role model for how I want to work with my staff. I'm pushed to think of new ways of doing things, which is good for me.
>
> I realize that this job is not perfect. I'd like my boss not to have a boss so that all decisions could be made at her level, and I'd like to hire a few more people in my area. But I wouldn't trade the feeling I have here. I know the big picture, where I fit, when and where to get help, and I know that I can trust my boss. She's no game player—she's an enlightened manager who believes in partnering with her staff and other managers. I also know that I work best in the environment that I'm in.

A Manager's Role in a Partnership

A partnership between a manager and an employee can happen only when each sees the other's value to the organization. Each needs to respect the other's talents and look for opportunities to put those talents to work. Creating awareness and forming alliances are the manager's responsibility. In turn, an aware employee brings a necessary ingredient to the alliance.

Before building partnerships, partnering managers distinguish among the roles involved in a collaborative approach. Partnering managers involve employees in decision making and interact regularly with them. Partnering managers provide direction, determine mutual goals, identify performance criteria and scope of authority, give feedback, solicit information and ideas, and discuss and provide needed resources. Partnering managers assume many roles as they interact with employees, as shown in Figure 6. They act in any of the following roles:

Figure 6. The Roles of a Partnering Manager

- **Coach** when encouraging excellence;
- **Trainer** when developing skills;
- **Model** when demonstrating appropriate behaviors;
- **Facilitator** when guiding the process;
- **Leader** when providing vision and direction; and
- **Evaluator** when appraising results.

Partnering managers move in and out of these roles as they interact with their employees in the work environment. They choose roles based on the situation and on employees' needs.

For example, a manager might begin the day by orienting a group of new employees, thus functioning as a trainer. During a meeting with a task force charged with solving a work flow problem, the manager may serve as a facilitator. Later in the day, he or she conducts a mid-year performance review and assumes the role of evaluator. In this typical scenario, the manager shifts from trainer to facilitator to evaluator in the course of one day, assuming the role appropriate to each situation. At times, the shifting is more frequent and might actually occur within one of the activities. For instance, redirecting the task force's effort would have required the manager to shift into a leadership role.

Figure 7 lists each role a partnering manager assumes and describes some typical behaviors.

The Employee's Role in a Partnership

A participatory environment requires that managers not underestimate their employees' capabilities. Employees initiate action, provide ideas, and practice self-management. In addition, they are responsible for being open and honest, for supporting new ideas, for learning new skills and information, and for offering suggestions and feedback.

ROLE	BEHAVIORS
Coach	Provides growth opportunities Provides corrective feedback Reinforces good performance Challenges the individual
Trainer	Assesses training and development needs Provides skill development Evaluates skill mastery Evaluates training transfer to the job
Model	Demonstrates appropriate partnering behaviors and techniques Demonstrates the performance expected of employees Responds to questions about the demonstrated behaviors
Facilitator	Assists partners with problem-solving, opportunity-seeking processes Ensures that partners remain in the roles established
Leader	Communicates vision Secures commitment Plans, implements, and evaluates changes Empowers others
Evaluator	Observes and documents work performed Assesses the quality of the work Assesses the quantity of the work Conducts performance-review sessions

Figure 7. Roles and Behaviors of a Partnering Manager

Partnering employees also provide the energy and enthusiasm vital to problem solving and opportunity seeking. Their focus is to improve and to strengthen their organizations. When interacting with their managers, partnering employees practice behaviors that enhance their partnering relationships. Figure 8 lists some typical manager-employee interactions and suggested partnering-employee behaviors.

In addition to the partnering behaviors expected in the manager-employee relationship, employees may be required to assume any of the managerial roles identified earlier as they do their jobs and work toward organizational change. For instance, an employee may be asked to train a new hire or to facilitate a new task-force meeting. Within or outside of the manager-employee relationship, partnering employees assume responsibility for their interactions, choosing behaviors that enhance partnering.

Partnering offers a chance for a win-win outcome. Employees at all levels are empowered to initiate and to create change, benefiting themselves, their departments, and their businesses.

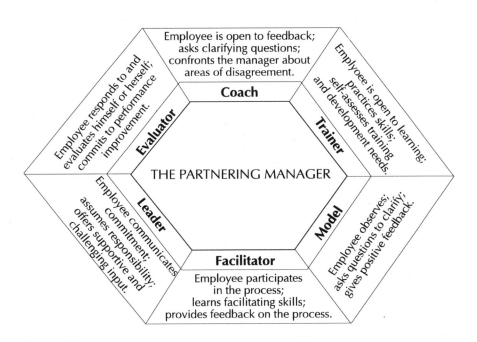

**Figure 8. Interactions Between a Partnering Manager
and a Partnering Employee**

Partnering employees want to solve problems and look for opportunities for personal and business growth. Enlightened by employees' ideas and input, managers are well positioned to move the business ahead. Dynamic partners want to stay on the competitive edge and become leaders in the corporate world.

Creating the Manager-Employee Partnership

Partnering will work only if managers create and support a participatory culture, one in which employees become involved in their work and in the decision-making process. When managers commit to a participatory culture, they become partnering managers who support the following beliefs:

- People are our most valuable resource.
- Each person brings something unique to the workplace.
- People prefer challenging work.
- People need and deserve to be involved in decisions that affect them.

To create a partnering culture, managers recognize employees need more than basic skills to perform their jobs effectively. Employees need to know how to partner with their managers and with one another. Partnering managers equip their employees with information, skills, authority, and resources. Each of these elements enhances the partnership process.

The partnering practices shown in Figure 9 build the foundation for manager-employee partnerships. Based on vision, commitment, and action, an application of these practices equips managers to build partnerships that work.

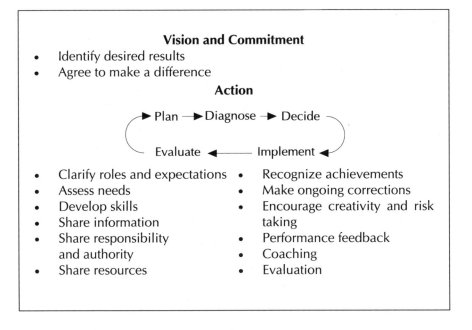

Figure 9. Partnering Practices for Successful Manager-Employee Partnering

Vision and Commitment

Partnering is a process. Although partnerships move through phases of development, the following partnering techniques and behaviors are employed throughout the partnership. Partnering is a powerful process that is results oriented and that involves behaviors of continuous monitoring, improvement, sharing, decision making, achievement, creativity, and recognition.

Identify desired results. Partnering managers believe in the value of shared vision, clear direction, and input from all levels. A partnering manager develops a clear, strategic direction and gains commitment by involving employees in the process of setting goals collectively and pursuing them actively.

Agree to make a difference. This sets the tone for a high-achieving partnership.

Action

Planning

Clarify Roles and Expectations

Partnering managers ensure that employees know what is expected of them. Using direct language and specific terms, they make certain that their employees understand tasks, responsibilities, preferred methods, and scheduled deadlines. Partnering managers involve employees in the setting of expectations. They know that employees can contribute important information about realistic, expected outcomes. Partnering managers solicit employee input in determining tasks, responsibilities, preferred methods, and schedules.

Setting performance expectations. The partners must review regularly what is expected of the employee (that is, acceptable levels of performance) in every area of responsibility of the employee's job. Most organizations dictate that this will happen once or twice a year; partnering managers, however, make this an ongoing activity.

Setting expectations involves establishing ways of measuring performance. When managers and employees decide on the criteria they will use to measure performance, the following guidelines will prove to be beneficial:

1. Set expectations that are realistic—ones that are within the employee's capabilities yet remain challenging.
2. Be specific; expectations must be clearly stated and well defined.

3. Establish measurability by stating a concrete behavior or expected outcome, including time limits, whenever appropriate.
4. Involve employees directly in establishing the expectations.

A manager-employee partnership might be free to determine the expectations for the employee. However, in large organizations with many employees holding similar jobs that are graded within a job classification system, performance expectations may need to be created by groups of managers working with groups of employees.

The following example describes a situation in which a manager and an employee independently determine a performance expectation.

Juanita and Jean, a manager-employee partnership within a bank, meet to set the standards for processing checks. They determine that the average employee can process a specific number of checks during a regular shift. Juanita and Jean then decide on acceptable performance for Jean by defining quality and quantity in clear, specific terms. They decide that Jean should process the specified number with no more than one percent error during the eight-hour shift. Together, Juanita and Jean decide if this is realistic. Are all the machines working properly to avoid delay or increased errors? Are the bundles easily accessible to the processor? Does Jean have other responsibilities that might interfere with her processing that number of checks? Once the things that could prevent Jean from meeting the performance expectation have been identified and corrected, both Juanita and Jean can agree on the expectations to use for measuring performance. As partners, they set expectations that are fair and they agree that the work will be performed in a particular way.

When specifying expected results, all partners should feel comfortable. Partnering managers and employees know what to measure and what to expect. This ensures that there will be no surprises at evaluation time. The employee will already know if his or her performance has exceeded or failed to meet the expected results.

In contrast to the previous situation, the following example describes how a large multinational company sets standards for large groups of employees holding similarly graded positions.

> Managers and nonexempt staff created a ten-person task force to review nonexempt job descriptions and to write performance expectations for each position. The task force reviewed various levels of support personnel, such as secretary, receptionist, mail clerk, and administrative assistant. Task-force members collected feedback on the performance expectations from other nonexempt and management employees. Working steadily for three months, they produced a set of expectations for each nonexempt position. The human resources department then reviewed the standards. To account for special assignments or responsibilities that differed from other jobs in the same job class, each individual partner-team was expected to develop three to five additional expectations.

Sample performance expectations. The following examples suggest performance expectations that are realistic, specific, and measurable:

- Handles telephone calls courteously and efficiently, responding to inquiries when appropriate and taking complete messages when a staff member is unavailable.
- Welds all types of polypropylene, polyethylene, CPVC, PVC, and Kynar, while following requirements for temperatures, welding tips, welding equipment, and elements.
- Wears safety equipment when required and reports hazards and unsafe conditions to immediate supervisor.
- Completes all receiving operation procedures: receives deliveries, unloads deliveries when required, checks materials received against invoices, signs receiving slips, forwards slips to the proper individuals, and stores the received materials appropriately.

Partnering managers involve employees in setting expectations for the following reasons:

- To demonstrate respect for employees as individuals;
- To recognize that employees know some things about their jobs that no one else may know;
- To provide an opportunity for managers to understand the obstacles employees face in their jobs; and
- To reduce resistance from employees. When employees see that they are partners and have been a part of the expectation-setting process, they feel a stronger commitment to the partnership and to achieving the expectations that were mutually established.

When a company determines its strategic direction, it looks at a plan for getting there. It then depends on its employees to take primary responsibility for implementing the plan. To do so efficiently, employees must know what is expected of them individually. Performance planning sets the strategic plan in motion.

Diagnosing, Decision Making, and Implementation

Diagnosing and making decisions are ongoing activities among partners. Committed to a shared vision, partners continually collect and analyze information related to their goals and make decisions based on the desired results. During diagnosing, partnering managers determine and review several courses of action with their employees. They examine the rationale—the benefits and the risks behind each option. The partners should agree on a course of action before working out specific details for implementation.

In a systematic approach the partners take the following actions:

- Collect pertinent data around an issue, problem, or opportunity;
- Determine possible modes of action;
- Challenge one another with questions;

- Encourage creativity and are willing to take risks based on data;
- Create a plan of action, outlining costs, time schedules, risks, and gains; and
- Document their decisions.

Assess Needs

The partnering manager identifies employees' needs and is sensitive to those needs. Employees need information, skills, resources, and the authority to do their jobs effectively. They also need a stimulating environment that helps them to maximize their potentials. A partnering manager accepts the responsibility and the challenge of knowing the needs of his or her staff. This means that the manager listens and reacts to employees consistently.

Once managers have recognized employees' needs, they differentiate those they can and cannot meet. Partnering managers who cannot meet employees' needs have options. They can offer an alternative, provide a portion of that need, or explain why a need cannot be met. Partnering managers always acknowledge requests and clarify whether or not those requests can be met. Understanding managers can feel uncomfortable turning down requests. Unfortunately, they then may avoid explaining their positions to employees. Partnering managers do everything in their power to respond to and to satisfy employees' workplace needs.

Develop Skills

Developing skills and ensuring skill transfer is much like sharing ideas. As technology and operational changes occur, partnering managers ensure that their employees have the skills needed to handle these changes. They strive to anticipate the job skills that will be needed and to provide opportunities for skill attainment, either inside or outside the organization. Partnering managers ensure that training occurs and that it focuses on current and future job skills as well as partnership development.

Partnering employees also have responsibilities. They need to assess their own skill deficiencies and see where they need development. When partnering employees request training, partnering managers evaluate those requests and respond appropriately. Partnering employees must possess the skills necessary for high-quality participation in the partnership. Skills that enhance partnering include problem-solving skills, change skills, communication skills, and interpersonal skills.

Problem-solving skills, such as identifying and defining a problem or opportunity; exploring and selecting courses of action; and implementing an action plan and tracking results.

Change skills, including recognizing the need for change; identifying the stages of the change process; and managing themselves and others through the change.

Communication skills, such as active listening; sensitivity to nonverbal behaviors; presenting ideas effectively; and good business writing.

Interpersonal skills, including recognizing and demonstrating appropriate social behaviors; working with different interpersonal styles; appreciating the uniqueness of others; and managing conflict.

By developing partnering skills, managers and employees are better equipped to participate in their own skill development. This training and development process is ongoing, thereby arming the work force with skills for the future as well as for the present. The keys to effective communication include self-assessment and growth.

Share Information

Most problems within organizations can be traced to breakdowns in communication. When a company is large and decentralized, communication becomes even more difficult. As businesses grow, so does the need for clear and timely ways to share information.

Most employees, like managers, want to be informed of what is happening in their organizations. They need to know where a company is going, what its goals are, what obstacles it has to overcome, and what opportunities exist. If managers do not convey information, the grapevine does, and grapevine information may well be distorted. This type of information sharing harms partnering efforts because trust between managers and employees is a critical ingredient for success. The more information managers share with those around them, the better informed the organization becomes as a whole. Although some information must be kept confidential (such as the possible termination of a senior-level manager), intentionally withholding information that could be shared destroys trust. Partnerships are more effective when both partners know what to expect when they share ideas and information and when they communicate ideas to others. The information flow is constant, moving upward, downward, and across the organization. When information is honest, clear, concise, and timely, there are no surprises and all partners operate from the same knowledge base.

Partnering managers communicate through one-on-one and group sessions, memos, bulletins, newsletters, annual reports, policies and procedures, task groups, and work teams.

Share Responsibility and Authority

Information and skills alone cannot make the partnership totally functional. Having increased information and skills, employees are ready for more responsibility and may well expect it. In effective partnerships, managers and employees share the responsibility for getting the job done in the best way possible. This sharing of responsibility brings with it a sharing of authority. This does not reduce the partnering manager's authority or clout. It does, however, mean that partnering employees are empowered with the authority needed to meet their responsibilities.

Partnering managers include employees in decisions that directly affect and/or relate to the management of their work. Partnering managers and employees continually make decisions about the opportunities open to them and about problems that need to be solved. The greater the employee responsibility in the decision-making process, the higher the level of his or her participation in the outcome, and the higher the investment in the organization.

Even in a participatory culture, managers make decisions without employees. When they do, they may request information from employees without sharing the reasons for needing it and without involving them in the final decision. However, when managers share the reasons for needing information and when they solicit employee ideas, they involve employees more although they still make the final decision. Both scenarios are acceptable in the participatory mode, providing the manager does not rely almost exclusively on making decisions without employee input.

Partnering managers are committed to functioning with as much participation as possible. They involve their employees in decisions that affect employees' jobs or the quality of their work life. Their management roles require them to make choices about when and where to use involvement techniques. Partnering managers identify appropriate opportunities for decision making with employees. Partnering managers share authority and may follow a course of action different from what they would have decided on their own, using the highest level of involvement appropriate for the decisions to be made.

At the end of this chapter is a checklist entitled "How Much Involvement?" Partnering managers may wish to use this checklist when considering the optimum level of employee involvement in decision making. A second checklist, "Should You Have Been Involved?" is a tool to assess how employees perceive the level of involvement that they had in a project. These checklists can also serve as a teaching tool for managers to use with staff members who might also need to involve others in decisions.

Share Resources

In addition to sharing information, skills, and authority, manager-employee partnerships share resources to accomplish mutual goals. Teamwork and productivity can fall by the wayside if the resources to do the work are not available. Those responsible for completing the work need to know where to get the resources that they need. If one partner controls the resources and shares only what he or she must share, the partnership will be damaged. The partnership may even be damaged beyond repair if one partner holds back resources intentionally and inappropriately.

Providing partners with information, skills, authority, and resources empowers them. This puts a company in a strong position to create new products, services, systems, and a better work environment. Partnering is an action process. It improves the business and the people within it, creating a "win-win" situation for all. Partnering managers play key roles in the creation of win-win environments.

Recognize Achievements

Managers who want dynamic partnerships nurture those partnerships by recognizing achievers. They catch employees doing something right and recognize them for doing so. Partnering managers tell employees when they notice their efforts. Although many managers recognize the need to reward achievers, only partners do it continually. Partnering managers also identify appropriate ways to recognize employees, including verbal recognition, written recognition (such as in the organization's newsletter or in a letter to top management), recognition at a meeting, or initiating employee-of-the-month programs.

Make Ongoing Corrections

Avoiding confrontations and failing to deal with issues when they occur can lead to greater problems in the future. Knowing about problems as they occur gives employees the opportunity to correct the problems and to move forward. Employees generally would rather not operate under the misconception that things are fine, only to find out differently later. Partnering managers use a "no-surprises" approach.

Encourage Creativity and Risk Taking

Partnering managers provide an environment that encourages creativity and risk taking. They learn to expect and even to accept occasional failure. If employees try new ways of doing their work, it stands to reason that sometimes their attempts will not be successful. If employees are supported in an analysis of what went wrong, they can learn from these experiences and can move confidently ahead to future challenges. Partnering managers succeed because their analyses are not threatening to employees. They seek to describe what went wrong not to place blame, but in the spirit of learning from the experience.

Partnering managers are open to ideas and alternative ways of looking at problems. Partners challenge one another to explore new ideas, to formulate alternative actions, and to brainstorm new approaches. This models an interest in and acceptance of change. Employees then feel free to explore new opportunities and are encouraged to do so.

Performance Feedback and Evaluation

Performance Feedback

Managers and employees both are responsible for assessing needs and for using performance expectations as a guide for evaluating daily work. Expected results should be the yardsticks on which to evaluate how well an employee is doing. Partnering managers and employees use mutually developed expectations as tools for discussing performance on a regular basis. These performance discussions are for the purpose of coaching employees, sharing observations, documenting work performed, evaluating performance, and planning development.

Partnering managers develop feedback techniques that support the manager-employee partnership. A number of tools exist that support coaching, evaluation, and documentation and strengthen the partnership.

Coaching

As coaches, partnering managers encourage and help partners to achieve mutually set goals and objectives. Coaching employees is similar to coaching athletes or musicians. Effective coaches encourage excellence by helping employees to set high but realistic goals. They push individuals to maximize their potentials. They praise successes and use failures as learning experiences. Coaches know the unique qualities of their performers and help them to build on their strengths. They attempt to provide the environment that will motivate people.

When partnering managers coach, they understand that motivation is an internal process. They ask themselves, "What motivates the performer?" Most people are motivated by basic things. They want some or all of the following:

- To work on challenging assignments;
- To have responsibility and authority over what they do;
- To be treated fairly;
- To be appreciated;
- To know that what they do is of value;
- To feel important;
- To feel needed;

- To do a good job and to be recognized for it; and
- To be able to make a difference.

As coaches, partnering managers create a positive atmosphere in which employees can feel that their needs are being met. Partnering managers coach employees in the following ways:

- By sharing ideas and information;
- By providing training and development;
- By being available when needed;
- By providing resources, assistance, and support;
- By demonstrating new tasks or equipment; and
- By seeking feedback, input, and ideas.

In the coaching role, partnering managers spend one-on-one private time with each employee. This private coaching session is a two-way communication between manager and employee. In a true partnership, the employee feels as free to request meetings as the manager does.

Coaching sessions provide ongoing guidance and support to employees. Such sessions may be scheduled to check progress toward expected results, to provide recognition, to solve problems, to encourage exemplary performance, to plan for development, or to set priorities for tasks. Coaching sessions may also occur spontaneously when a manager observes exceptional or poor quality work. Both the scheduled and spontaneous sessions are more than quick "pat-on-the-back" recognition meetings. Although feedback is necessary and even encouraged in a partnering relationship, true coaching sessions have more substance. They occur in private places, are initiated by the manager or employee, and are documented so that they can be referred to later in evaluation sessions. At least three to five such sessions should occur between partnering managers and employees within a year. New partnerships may call for as many as one or two sessions weekly.

When coaching sessions are scheduled ahead of time, they give managers and employees advance notice that a performance-related discussion will occur. Sometimes events require that sessions be held immediately. For example, if an individual shared a great idea at a meeting that would clearly solve an existing problem, a follow-up conversation might be highly motivating for him or her. When an employee displays inappropriate behavior, an immediate session should be called with the employee to discuss the inappropriate behavior, potential consequences if it continues, and alternatives to replace the inappropriate behavior. Tools for guiding partnering managers through a mutually beneficial coaching discussion are provided at the end of this chapter.

A partnering employee who wishes to speak with the manager on a performance-related issue should be encouraged to initiate a coaching session. For example, an employee cannot meet a deadline because he or she has not received a report from accounting. After repeated attempts to get the report, it becomes the responsibility of the employee to initiate a session with his or her manager. It then becomes the manager's responsibility to make certain that the report gets to the employee with enough time to finish the job and to meet the deadline. In such a coaching session, the employee and the manager seek to improve an existing situation. Taking notes during the session provides records of the discussion and the eventual outcome, which can be valuable as a reference later.

Employees are strongly encouraged to request coaching sessions with their managers. This demonstrates a commitment to the partnership and also to their responsibilities for functioning as partnering employees. If an employee initiates a session to ask for help, direction, or information, the partnering manager strives for the following objectives:

- To make the employee feel comfortable;
- To listen to the purpose of the session as the employee describes it;
- To probe for more information, if needed;
- To work to solve the problem mutually and to develop a plan for action; and
- To suggest a follow-up session to see how things are going.

A partnering manager wisely keeps notes on the coaching sessions, which serve the following purposes:

- To provide a record of discussions for both the manager and the employee;
- To communicate to the employee that coaching discussions for recognition and correction are important;
- To serve as a reminder to follow up when necessary;
- To help to prepare for evaluation sessions; and
- To provide performance documentation.

A partnering manager creates useful documentation for future reference. Tools for documenting coaching sessions are provided at the end of this chapter.

Evaluation

Many managers think that they do a thorough job of evaluating performance. However they often give lip service to the process and rush through it to meet end-of-the-year deadlines. Rather than being a partnership effort that is designed with input from all levels within the company, evaluation becomes an annual activity grudgingly performed to make the boss or the personnel department happy.

Evaluation determines whether or not what was expected actually took place. Therefore evaluation is not just a once-a-year activity to be dreaded by all involved. A partnership effort requires a very different approach to evaluation: It becomes a part of the manager's everyday responsibility. Evaluation is based on the performance planning that was done at the beginning of the period to be evaluated and is a compilation of the coaching discussions that were held with the employee throughout the year. In this way, the annual evaluation session summarizes the employee's efforts for the past year and opens the door to a new year, allowing the partners to set new expectations based on the organization's strategic direction.

Managers may want to conduct a two-part session, with the evaluation or assessment piece occurring at one point and the future expectations and developmental planning portion done at another point.

A partnering manager, operating in a highly participative mode, structures the formal evaluation discussion as follows:

1. A review of expectations;
2. A review of significant accomplishments;
3. A development plan for the future; and
4. A determination of the next year's expectations.

The manager who wishes to strengthen the partnering relationship ensures that he or she and the employee are prepared for the session. The following guidelines may be helpful for the manager.

Determine when to get help outside the team. Even though managers form partnerships with their employees, they need to recognize when support and assistance from outside the team are necessary. When problems arise that partners cannot solve, they need to look to those who have the resources and ability to help. This does not hinder managers' partnering with their staff members; it actually supports partnering. Ignoring the need to go outside the team for help can be frustrating for everyone involved. Managers may fear that employees will perceive them as lacking competence if they request help. Instead they should realize that employees respect managers who understand the team's limitations. When managers see the need for help, they must intervene and secure assistance. This support can come from another manager or from an inside or outside consultant.

Assess results. During implementation, partners examine the checkpoints that were established during the planning phase. At these checkpoints, the partners evaluate the effectiveness of the relationship and the overall results. They decide if they are truly achieving the changes that they had wanted originally. If they have become sidetracked or if their direction is unclear, they can make adjustments immediately, thereby averting failure and saving time and resources.

To evaluate the accomplishments, partners ask the following questions:

- What are the evidences of success?
- Are we on schedule? If not, why not?
- Are we working within our allotted resources? If not, why not?
- Have we been working smart, using the best methods possible? If not, how can we improve? What is the specific plan to do so?

Assess the partnership. To evaluate the partnership itself partners ask the following questions:

- What do we feel contributes to our ability to work well together?
- What hinders our working relationship?
- What might we do differently in the future?
- Are we upholding our commitments to one another?

One key advantage of evaluating outcomes periodically is that partners can identify any difficulty early on and can redirect their efforts. This not only saves time and money but also builds credibility for the partners. Evaluating helps partners to track their successes and provides vital information to their companies about where they have been, where they are going, and if they are traveling at the proper speed.

B & E Manufacturing—
Putting Manager-Employee
Partnerships to Work

Richard, a manager at B & E, wanted to start a wellness program. He considered hiring an external consultant to design a program that only he would review and collaborate on, thereby saving time and money. After learning about partnering, he realized that excluding employees meant running the risk of choosing a program that was unappealing to and unsupported by them.

Richard then considered a more involved process. He thought about asking the consultant to design the wellness program after assessing employee wants and needs. Obviously, the expense and time involved would increase, but there would be a higher likelihood of the program's being accepted by the employees. Richard finally decided to involve employees at a much broader level. He formed an employee task force to develop a wellness program. First, he established a partnership with a designated facilitator. The partners clarified their roles, expectations, and needs in terms of the partnership. Then they partnered with the task force.

The methods for assessing employee wants and needs and the final design of the program were in the hands of the task force. They were given a budget for the program and the resources to implement it for a one-year trial period. The effort took a bit longer, but the costs were less than they would have been if a consultant had been used. The amount of employee time needed to design the program was also greater; however, this highly participative approach enabled employees to view the program as truly theirs. By sharing a vision, committing to a joint enterprise, and acting collaboratively, Richard and his staff moved toward a successful outcome.

Throughout the project, they made conscious efforts to share information and decision-making responsibility. The decision-making process was not always in a problem-solving mode.

Richard and his employees continually made decisions while seeking opportunities. Although they may not have continuously operated at the highest levels of participation, partnering meant making the right choices about how the group should function. As a partnering manager, Richard used the highest level of involvement appropriate for the decisions to be made. He considered the optimum level of employee involvement in decision making and conducted assessments of how the employees perceived the level of involvement that they had in the project.

Summary

Although managers have the responsibility for managing staff, resources, and production, they cannot be all things to all people. Unfortunately, time, technology, and trends place demands on the manager, and even the smallest teams are forced to explore ways in which they can compete in today's and tomorrow's worlds. One sure way of meeting such needs is for the manager to form a partnership with staff members.

This partnership then becomes a life-sustaining part of daily operations. Managers involve employees in meeting the goals that the company sets. They provide the information that their partners need, the resources and skills required for the job, and the authority to carry it out. They provide an environment that supports and encourages participation. Moving from old ways of doing business, managers and employees partner to provide input to the problem-solving and opportunity-seeking processes.

Managers involve employees in the performance-planning process and in setting the expectations by which their performance will be measured. Through coaching, documenting, and evaluating performance, managers provide feedback as to how well employees are doing and areas in which they can improve.

Partners respect the value of employees' experiences; the value of involving employees in decisions related to their jobs; the value of challenging employees to reach higher expectations; and the value of recognizing employees' achievements.

Unfortunately, there is no magic in this. Partnering takes work, time, and a commitment to surpass what has been done in the past. A dedication to partnering pushes the organization forward. The partnering bond is often long-term and has the ability to empower managers and employees alike. They can reach places they have never gone before. The future looks bright! Partnership puts organizations on the competitive edge.

The following checklist provides a listing of the activities, considerations, and processes involved in partnering with employees. You could use this as an aid in planning, initiating, and developing partnerships.

Tools for coaching employees and for determining employee involvement in decision making follow this checklist.

1. ASSESS READINESS TO PARTNER.

- ☐ Do I consider people my most valuable resource?
- ☐ Do I perceive more benefits than problems when I ask people for their ideas, suggestions, and opinions?
- ☐ Do I see value in giving authority to those I supervise?
- ☐ Do I want all partners to define expected results together?
- ☐ Do I see value in providing regular performance feedback?

2. CREATE VISION AND COMMITMENT.

- ☐ Identify desired results.
- ☐ Develop a clear, strategic direction.
- ☐ Gain commitment by involving employees in setting goals collectively.
- ☐ Agree to make a difference.

3. TAKE ACTION.

- ☐ Clarify roles.
- ☐ Involve employees in the setting of expectations.
- ☐ Solicit employee input in determining tasks, responsibilities, preferred methods, and schedules.
- ☐ Assess needs.
- ☐ Determine needs that we can and cannot meet and respond appropriately.

- ☐ Provide current and future job skills training as well as partnership development.
- ☐ Provide information through one-on-one and group sessions, memos, bulletins, newsletters, annual reports, policies and procedures, task groups, and work teams.
- ☐ Share responsibility for getting the job done in the best way possible. Empower employees with the authority needed to meet their responsibilities.
- ☐ Include employees in decisions that relate to the management of their work. Share decisions about opportunities and problems that need to be solved.
  - ☐ Consider the optimum level of employee involvement in decision making using the tool found at end of this chapter.
  - ☐ Assess how employees perceive the level of involvement that they had in a project using the tool found at end of this chapter.
- ☐ Work with employees to determine needs and find resources.
- ☐ Recognize achievements in appropriate ways for the person and achievement: verbally, in publications, at meetings, through written forms/letters/certificates, or by employee-recognition programs.
- ☐ Correct problems before they become more serious.
- ☐ Encourage creativity and risk-taking behaviors. Challenge and stimulate one another.
- ☐ Evaluate progress (see the checklist in Chapter V).
- ☐ Determine when to get help outside the team.
- ☐ Assess results.
- ☐ Assess the partnership.

Conducting a Performance-Improvement Discussion

- Open the discussion by identifying the purpose of the meeting.
- Clarify the performance problem and ask about circumstances surrounding it.
- Give the employee balanced feedback by discussing the positive circumstances and the concerns related to the performance.
- Discuss ideas for keeping the positive aspects of the performance and for improving the areas of concern related to the performance.
- Agree on the specific actions that will be taken, summarize the meeting, and schedule a follow-up session.

Conducting a Performance-Recognition Discussion

- Open the discussion by identifying the purpose of the meeting.
- Describe the exemplary performance and the positive consequences of the performance as they affect the manager, the employee, and the organization.
- Ask for or give suggestions for continuing the performance.
- Communicate appreciation to the employee for performing above and beyond expectations.

Coaching-Session Summary

Employee's Name   Date
Position   Department

The Coaching Session Summary provides a guide and record for managers to document performance discussions with employees. To identify performance that exceeds or consistently meets expectations, only Sections I, II, and V need be completed. To identify poor performance areas, Sections I through V must be completed.

Section I: Observed Behavior or Performance. Write specific examples of behavior or performance that have been observed.

Section II: Employee's Comments.

Section III: Employee/Manager Suggestions.

Section IV: Action Plan (including training when appropriate).

Section V: Signatures.

Employee   Manager

How Much Involvement?

Instructions: Respond to the following questions. A large percentage of "yes" answers indicates that others should be mutually involved in the decision making.

	YES	NO
1. Do you need information related to this decision from others?	_____	_____
2. Are you willing to share information related to this decision with others?	_____	_____
3. Are you willing to consider opinions and ideas from others?	_____	_____
4. Does this decision directly affect others?	_____	_____
5. Do you have the time required to work through the decision with others?	_____	_____
6. Do others have the time required to work through the decision?	_____	_____
7. Do you have the resources required to work through the decision with others?	_____	_____
8. Do you need or want buy-in for the decision from others?	_____	_____
9. Are you willing to share your authority?	_____	_____
10. Are you committed to the follow-through necessary to implement the decision?	_____	_____

Should You Have Been Involved?

Instructions: Respond to the following questions. A large percentageof "yes" answers indicates that you should have been involved in the decision making.

	YES	NO
1. Do you have information related to the decision?	_____	_____
2. Were you willing to share information related to this decision?	_____	_____
3. Did you want to give your opinion?	_____	_____
4. Did this decision directly affect you and others with whom you work?	_____	_____
5. Did you have the time required to work through the decision with others?	_____	_____
6. Did others have the time required to work through the decision?	_____	_____
7. Did you have the resources required to work through the decision with others?	_____	_____
8. Did you buy in to the decision that was made?	_____	_____
9. Were you willing to share responsibility for the decision?	_____	_____
10. Were you committed to the follow-through necessary to implement the decision?	_____	_____

Chapter

V

PARTNERING
WITH CONSULTANTS

"Synergy is 1 + 1 = 3*"*

—R. Buckminster Fuller

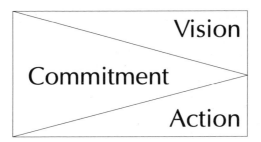

A major utility company planned to do some restructuring based on its new strategic focus. Senior management determined what the "new" organization would look like and planned to announce and to implement the changes within three months. The corporate human resources vice president was one of the decision makers. To facilitate the change, the vice president assigned staff members to partner with line managers at each site.

After examining their roles and skills, the human resource managers decided to seek the expertise of an external consultant. The vice president approved this decision. After choosing the consultant, the human resource managers requested a change-management workshop designed to train the human resource staff. In the workshop, the human resource staff members were challenged to examine their roles as change facilitators. The consultant then helped them to develop guidelines that outlined their responsibilities to the line managers throughout the change process. As a workshop instructor, the consultant contributed useful change-initiation and change-management techniques. The group profited from information about resistance to change as well as from the consultant's experience with different types of organizational change. The partnering efforts—internal partnering with line managers, internal partnering with external consultants, and external partnering with line managers—brought together a great deal of talent. New ideas emerged and a plan of action was designed to implement change effectively.

The human resource staff and line managers partnered well with one another and with the consultant to implement change effectively. Their efforts resulted in a smooth transition, and the techniques they learned proved invaluable to the company as it continued to grow and to change.

Sometimes partnering managers need to look beyond their partnerships for assistance. They may need a consultant to offer solutions through new ideas and methods. Whether they go outside the organization or look internally for support in their efforts, partnering managers must seek consultants whose skills best suit their needs.

The Role of a Consultant

Consultants are actually change agents. They analyze problems or opportunities and recommend courses of action. As is the case with manager-to-manager and manager-to-employee partnerships, partnerships with consultants improve the organization through constructive change.

Partnering managers recognize that consultants, internal (from within the company) or external (from outside the company), always work outside of the system in which they consult. If a consultant is unfamiliar with the system, the partnering manager introduces the consultant to the manager-employee partnership so that he or she can begin to work with that partnership.

Determining the Need for a Consultant

When deciding whether or not to hire a consultant, a manager should ask the following questions:

- Do we need more experience or ability than we currently have with our partnerships?
- Do we need someone who can devote more time than we can to the change effort?
- Do we need an objective, outside perspective?
- Can we learn from what others have done in this situation?

If the answer to any of these questions is "yes," the organization can benefit from finding an appropriate consultant. To enable the consulting relationship to work effectively, partnering managers should gain commitment from their employee partnership before engaging a consultant. Employees want to know why an outsider is needed and what the manager hopes to accomplish. Their buy-in brings their support, which is crucial to a successful change effort.

Because the project requires financial and organizational support during as well as after the change effort, partnering managers seek approval and commitment from the next level of management. Support from upper-level management can help to ensure the success of the endeavor.

An Internal Versus an External Consultant

If the first decision is whether or not to seek a consultant, the second decision is whether that consultant should come from inside or outside the organization. Figure 10 compares some of the advantages and disadvantages of internal and external consultants.

How To Select An Appropriate Consultant

When selecting a consultant, a partnering manager makes certain that the person is a skilled change agent and that he or she can partner effectively with the client. Partnering managers use the following guidelines to decide whether to bring in a consultant:

1. Outline the purpose(s) and scope of the project.
2. Identify the skills, information, experience, and resources—including time—that are necessary to accomplish the project.
3. Consider the advantages and disadvantages of internal and external consultants.
4. If it is more advantageous to use an internal consultant, assess the talents of internal staff members and make a list of

INTERNAL CONSULTANTS	
ADVANTAGES	**DISADVANTAGES**
Understand the organization's politics, budget constraints, and goals.	May have a biased approach or a limited range of experiences to bring to the partnership.
Are already working in the environment and know the policies and procedures.	May already have a preconceived notion of what works and what does not work.
Are committed to the organization and its strategic plan.	May be too threatened or influenced by top management, the manager, or their own managers to be objective.
Usually cost less than external consultants.	May be involved in other projects and unable to make a full-time commitment.
EXTERNAL CONSULTANTS	
ADVANTAGES	**DISADVANTAGES**
Can bring a fresh approach and varying experiences to the partnership.	May not know the environment, politics, budget constraints, goals, policies, procedures, or organizational background and may need to be given such information.
Have no preconceived notions about what works within the environment.	Are committed to the organization and its goals only from the standpoint of committing to the project and providing a service.
Are not threatened or influenced by members of the organization.	May cost more than internal consultants.
Can concentrate their energies on the project.	May be available with only long-term notice.

Figure 10. Choosing Between Internal and External Consultants

possible candidates. The following questions are appropriate to consider:

- Is there a planner within the partnership?
- What skills do other internal candidates have?
- Do candidates possess teaching or coaching skills?
- Are the candidates good communicators? Listeners? Speakers?

5. If it is more advantageous to use an external consultant, assess the qualifications of a number of consultants using the following guidelines:

- Get leads and make a list of possible candidates. Sources for leads include co-workers, outside colleagues, professional associations, advertisements, local universities, and/or consultants/authors whose work is respected and is related to the project.
- Select three to five consultants and contact them by telephone.
- Conduct general reference checks.
- Schedule interviews with those being considered.

6. Interview both internal and external candidates to evaluate their experience with similar projects and their successes and failures. In certain situations, it is appropriate to contact prior clients to corroborate information. Address the following topics:

- What was the consultant hired to do?
- Was it accomplished?
- Was it accomplished within the resources and time frame allotted?
- How did the consultant demonstrate competence and objectivity?
- What role(s) did the consultant play (adviser, facilitator, or trainer?)
- With whom did the consultant work directly?

- Would these people use the consultant again? Why or why not?
- Does the person offer leadership, assertiveness, and credibility?

7. Whether using an internal or an external consultant, consider the person's style and his or her willingness to partner, using the following guidelines:
   - Is the person flexible or rigid, an extrovert or an introvert, a partnership player or a loner?
   - How does the person deal with others? Is he or she open or brash?

8. Request proposals from internal and external candidates who seem to be good matches in terms of interest, ability, experience, resources, style, and willingness to partner.

9. Review the proposals to select the most appropriate consultant, using the following considerations:
   - The consultant's understanding of the problem;
   - The consultant's experience, ability, and resources;
   - The approach he or she suggests; and
   - The costs.

10. Select the consultant or consulting firm.

11. Notify the selected consultant and the other internal and external candidates who submitted proposals, making sure that all candidates receive replies.

12. Whether the consultant is external or internal, develop a letter of agreement. The agreement should detail the following information:
   - Services to be rendered;
   - The results expected;
   - The responsibilities of both the consultant and the manager;
   - The role(s) that the consultant is expected to assume and a description of expected partnering behaviors;

- Methods of evaluation, which will measure the success of the intervention, the expected results, the progress toward the desired result, and the effectiveness of the partnering behaviors;
- The consultant's fees and what the costs will include;
- Time lines showing intermediate deadline dates and a completion date for the entire project; and
- Conditions under which either party could terminate the partnership should circumstances warrant it.

Building A Partnership — Vision and Commitment

After selecting a consultant and signing an agreement, a partnering manager is ready to build the partnership. A partnering manager who contracts with a consultant is responsible for laying the foundation to build the manager-consultant partnership. The organization's resources and staff provide the support for the foundation, but the manager forms the bond that enables the partnership to succeed.

To solidify the relationship, partnering managers follow these basic guidelines:

Clearly communicate expectations on the subject of confidentiality. This aspect is essential for the consultant-manager partnership and the project to be successful. Make certain the consultant clearly understands exactly what information can be shared, when, and with whom. Even if a manager has explained these expectations during the selection process, they should be discussed again to avoid misunderstandings. At this point, the manager also explains the consequences of not adhering to these expectations.

Provide the consultant with the internal staff to do the work. Based on the letter of agreement that clarifies roles, responsibilities, benchmarks and deadlines, specify who will do what, when it will be done, and how it will be done. The partnering manager is responsible for upholding these commitments and for ensuring that staff and other employees do the same. Even if the manager appoints another manager or a task force to work with the consultant, he or she still needs to be part of the process.

Conduct meetings between the consultant and key internal people regularly. Partnering managers make certain that the organization's commitment, which was made at the time the consultant was hired, is evidenced throughout the project.

Explain the organization's culture to the consultant early in the partnership. Partnering managers take time to answer questions and to clarify information. Without a clear understanding of the culture within the organization, the consultant's efforts may be in vain. Managers in the company need to share information about values, norms, the way people interact within the organization, the relationship with competitors, the level of employee acceptance, and any other facts that will provide the consultant with a better understanding of the organization. This information needs to be accurate and unbiased.

Check to see that the organization is benefiting from the consultant's efforts. Inasmuch as the manager is key to the partnership's success, he or she is also responsible for results. From the onset, the manager and the other members of the partnership should benefit from the use of a consultant. That means that everyone involved becomes a part of the change process. Specifics of what to look for as the process continues are presented in Chapter VI, but the following list outlines the benefits to be expected from the intervention:

- The problem should become clear and separate from the symptoms.
- The opportunity should become focused, forming a vision that all can see.

- Managers and staff members should gain some assessment skills.
- Managers should be able to observe and to model partnering behaviors.
- The organization should see value in the objective, outside perspective.
- The client becomes empowered during and as a result of the consultation.

Always operate within the role(s) agreed on. The manager's role might be as a liaison between the consultant and the organization or as the key decision maker when recommendations are being made. It is important for the manager to adhere to agreed-on roles and to clarify any need for these roles to change.

A consultant could be used to clarify problems, to assess needs, to give advice, to offer expertise, or to facilitate focus groups or planning meetings. Unless the nature of the project dictates a change or unexpected events take place, agreed-on roles should be fulfilled.

Laying this foundation provides the partnership with the base it needs to develop and to move toward results. The effective manager-consultant partnership, like the effective manager-employee partnership, is a collaborative, win-win relationship.

Partnering managers play key roles in molding the manager-consultant partnership by preparing those who will be working with the consultant. The following model outlines the development of a manager-consultant partnership.

Assessing Readiness

Everyone who will be working directly or indirectly with the consultant needs to accept and to understand the consultant's assignment. To accomplish this, the manager can serve the following functions:

- To clarify and stress the need for absolute confidentiality;

- To provide adequate internal staffing;
- To set the stage for internal people to learn from the consultant;
- To share information about the organization and its culture with the consultant;
- To identify others who will share information about the organization; and
- To operate within the role(s) clarified and agreed on with the consultant.

Planning

In the planning phase, the manager and the consultant address the following tasks:

- To define the problem or opportunity in very specific terms, describing the conditions that created the problem(s) or provided the opportunities;
- To specify clear, expected results to ensure that the change effort will strengthen the organization;
- To restate agreed-on roles and to discuss the behaviors necessary to carry them out; and
- To review other commitments in the letter of agreement, such as methods of diagnosis, benchmarks and deadlines, resources needed, and methods of evaluation.

Diagnosing

In the manager-consultant partnership, the consultant's role usually is to diagnose. In this phase, consultants work within the organization to gather the information that provides the basis for their analyses and recommendations. This collection of factual, unbiased information is critical to a thorough analysis. Most consultants use a variety of methods, including direct observations, surveys or questionnaires, interviews, and/or reviews of existing data (such as strategic plans or performance evaluations).

This diagnosis phase is greatly affected by how readily the consultants are accepted by those being observed, surveyed, or interviewed. Again, the partnering manager plays a key role in preparing people within the organization. Acceptance of the consultant may also be based on what happened during previous consultations. Employees may not be very candid if confidentialities were breached or if they perceive that nothing productive came from earlier recommendations.

Recommending

In the manager-consultant partnership, the consultant is the one expected to offer recommendations. These recommendations should be presented as specified in the planning phase. The ideal format is for the consultant to give recommendations to the manager orally and in writing. In this way, the manager can clarify issues around a particular recommendation and can use the written report for future reference.

Partnering managers may also request that the consultant suggest several possible courses of action. Often a consultant can provide an "ideal" plan but also can offer recommendations that might be more efficient in terms of time or cost. Before a manager can select an alternative recommendation, he or she needs to assess trade-offs, i.e., the rationale behind each recommendation, its benefits, and its risks, if any. Effective, objective, and ethical consultants can substantiate recommendations based on their diagnoses. The manager and the consultant should agree on a course of action before the consultant works out specific details for the implementation phase.

In a systematic approach the manager can expect the consultant to do the following:

- To summarize the information gathered in the diagnosis phase;

- To explain how the information that was gathered led to the recommendations;
- To provide a detailed plan of action that outlines costs, time schedules, risks, and gains;
- To answer questions; and
- To include a written document as a resource to be used during and after the meeting.

A manager may need time to consider the recommendations before discussing an implementation plan or may choose to discuss recommendations with employees, other managers, supervisors, or boards of directors. Successful implementation occurs with high buy-in and commitment from all concerned.

Implementing

The consultant's involvement in the implementation process is determined in the planning phase. If the consultant does not have the skills needed to participate in this phase, the partners should seek additional expertise. A partnering consultant will provide a detailed plan of what needs to be done, by whom, and in what sequence. The partnering manager is responsible for taking action.

Evaluating

A partnering manager's key concern is that the change effort resulting from the consultation makes the organization better rather than just different. Methods of evaluation are established in the planning phase. The partnering manager sees that they are carried out during the project and at its conclusion.

A key question during the project is "Are we progressing toward the goals we set?" A key question at the conclusion of the project is "Did we meet expected results?" The manager looks at time lines to determine if they are being met and at resources to determine if they are being used effectively.

In addition to reviewing progress toward results, a partnering manager also evaluates the use of partnering behaviors. At the onset, managers and consultants determine the behaviors they intend to demonstrate. Truly effective partners evaluate their own relationship, because the success of the project is influenced by whether or not true partnering occurred.

More information about evaluation techniques and tools is presented in the next chapter.

Examples of Partnering Situations

Small Business Owner and External Consultant

The owner of a small business that was grossing $800,000 wanted to develop a strategic plan for expanding the business. Based on where the owner wanted to be in three years, he searched for and found a consultant who understood his goal and who had had similar successes in the past. Together they began a partnership that moved the business toward the desired growth.

The partnership blossomed from the beginning. As business owner and consultant worked toward a clearly stated goal, the consultant empowered the owner by teaching him planning skills and guiding him in the implementation of a strategic plan. By learning the business and researching the competition, the consultant developed a clear understanding of the project's parameters. The consultant's plan was to provide the client with what they had agreed on: a clear path to achieve gross sales of $1.5 million within the next three years.

By the end of the formal partnership, the owner understood how to go about achieving his goal and was confident that he would do so. The consultant also became a valuable resource for the future. A partnership that was to be short-term evolved into a long-term relationship.

President and External Consultant

After reading about participative management and its effects on productivity, the president of a company with about 3,000 employees called in a consultant. He wanted his organization to become more participative. The consultant soon realized that the president's values and beliefs did not support such a change.

When the consultant presented the types of changes the company would have to make to move it from a highly autocratic environment to a very involved participative one, the president became nervous. He was used to "pushing employees harder so they would do better," and "making certain that employees worked for their pay." Unless the president could change his own thinking, he could not hope to change the work environment.

Over the next six to eight months, the president did some serious thinking. It took him eighteen months to be ready to form a partnership with the consultant. By then, he was committed to the kinds of behaviors he and his staff would need to practice in order to change the company's culture.

Within a two-year period, employees and managers saw a better quality of work life, and the company experienced a significant increase in profits. Senior managers asserted that the partnership approach played a key role in these results.

Had the president tried to enter into a partnership with the consultant before changing his thinking and making a commitment to participatory management, the project would have failed.

Organizational Development Director and External Consultant

Maria, chief executive officer (CEO) of a hospital, sought the services of an external consultant to help her interact better with her senior staff. Because problems existed between Maria and two of her four vice presidents, the organization development director, John, suggested hiring an external consultant.

John prescreened several well-known and respected local consultants and sent recommendations to Maria. As a result, she hired Gene and eventually formed a long-term partnership with his firm.

As Maria's partnership with Gene grew, her partnership with John suffered. Inadvertently, she had become too dependent on Gene, utilizing him for projects that would normally have been assigned to John. When John approached Maria about this issue, she responded well to his concerns. They worked together to determine when it might be more advantageous to use him or to use the consultant. In doing so, Maria and John learned a valuable lesson. Should a long-term partnership evolve with an external consultant, all would benefit from a thorough understanding of their individual roles.

Summary

Managers may find that partnering with a consultant can benefit their teams. Sometimes using an internal consultant is best; other times securing help from outside the organization is a better approach. Regardless of whether the manager's choice is internal or external, using a consultant is wise, especially when managers need special expertise or full-time attention to their problems or opportunities. Partnering with managers, consultants should focus on achieving results and strengthening the organization. Making the right match even in a short-term partnership could create a measurable business advantage.

The following can be used as a work sheet for determining the need for a consultant as well as to prepare to partner with a consultant. It is also useful in the process of developing and managing partnerships with consultants.

1. DETERMINE THE NEED FOR A CONSULTANT

- ☐ Do we need more experience or ability than we currently have in the partnership?
- ☐ Do we need someone who can devote more time than we can to the change effort?
- ☐ Do we need an objective, outside perspective?
- ☐ Can we learn from what others have done in this situation?

2. SELECT AN APPROPRIATE CONSULTANT

- ☐ Outline the purpose(s) and scope of the project.
- ☐ Identify what skills, information, experience, and resources, including time, are necessary to accomplish the project.
- ☐ Consider the advantages and disadvantages of internal and external consultants.
- ☐ If it is more advantageous to use an internal consultant, consider the talents of internal staff and make a list of possible candidates.
  - ☐ Is there a planner within the partnership?
  - ☐ What kinds of skills do other internal candidates have?
  - ☐ Do the candidates possess teaching or coaching skills?
  - ☐ Are they good communicators? Listeners? Speakers?
- ☐ If it is more advantageous to use an external consultant, consider the qualifications of a number of consultants.

☐ Get leads and make a list of possible candidates.

☐ Select three to five consultants and contact them by telephone.

☐ Conduct general reference checks.

☐ Schedule interviews with those being considered.

☐ Interview both internal and external candidates to evaluate their experience with similar projects and their successes and failures.

    ☐ What was the consultant hired to do?

    ☐ Was it accomplished?

    ☐ Was it accomplished within the resources and time frame allotted?

    ☐ How did the consultant demonstrate competence and objectivity?

    ☐ What role(s) did the consultant play (adviser, facilitator, or trainer?)

    ☐ With whom did the consultant work directly?

    ☐ Would these people use the consultant again? Why or why not?

    ☐ Does the person offer leadership, assertiveness, and credibility?

Note: In the case of external consultants, a manager may choose to contact prior clients to corroborate the preceding questions.

☐ Whether using an internal or an external consultant, consider his or her style and willingness to partner.

    ☐ Is he or she flexible or rigid, extroverted or introverted, a partner or a loner?

    ☐ How does he or she deal with others? Is he or she open or brash?

☐ Request proposals from both external and internal candidates who seem to be good matches in terms of interest, ability, experience, resources, style, and willingness to partner.

☐ Review the proposals to select the most appropriate consultant. Consider:

  ☐ The consultant's understanding of the problem.

  ☐ The suggested approach.

  ☐ The consultant's experience, ability, and resources.

  ☐ The costs.

☐ Select the consultant or consulting firm.

☐ Notify the selected consultant and the other internal and external candidates who submitted proposals. Partnering managers reply to all candidates.

☐ Whether the consultant is internal or external, develop a letter of agreement.

3. CLARIFY VISION AND COMMITMENT

☐ Clearly communicate expectations on the subject of confidentiality.

☐ Provide the consultant with the internal staff to do the work, using the letter of agreement that clarifies roles, responsibilities, benchmarks, and deadlines—including who will do what, when it will be done, and how.

☐ Conduct regular meetings between the consultant and key internal people.

☐ Explain the organization's culture to the consultant early in the partnership.

☐ Check to see that the organization is benefiting from the consultant's efforts.

☐ The problem should become clear and separate from the symptoms.

☐ The opportunity should become focused, forming a vision that all can see.

☐ Managers and staff should gain some assessment skills.

☐ Managers should be able to observe and to model partnering behaviors.

☐ The organization should see value in the objective, outside perspective.

☐ Always operate within the agreed-on roles.

4. TAKE ACTION

☐ Assess readiness between managers and consultants.

    ☐ Clarify and stress the need for absolute confidentiality.

    ☐ Provide adequate internal staff.

    ☐ Set the stage for internal people to learn from the consultant.

    ☐ Share information about the organization and its culture with the consultant.

    ☐ Identify others who will share information about the organization.

    ☐ Operate within the role(s) clarified and agreed on with the consultant.

☐ Conduct planning between managers and consultants.

    ☐ Define the problem or opportunity in very specific terms. Describe the conditions that created the problem(s) or provided the opportunities.

    ☐ Define clear, expected results to ensure that the change effort will strengthen the organization.

    ☐ Restate agreed-on roles and discuss behaviors expected to carry them out.

    ☐ Review other commitments in the letter of agreement such as the following:

        ☐ Methods of diagnosis

        ☐ Benchmarks and deadlines

        ☐ Resources needed

        ☐ Methods of evaluation

☐ Perform diagnosis.

☐ Review recommendations.

☐ The manager can expect the partnering consultant to do the following:

   ☐ Summarize the information gathered in the diagnosis phase.

   ☐ Explain how the information that was gathered led to the recommendations.

   ☐ Provide a detailed plan of action, outlining costs, time schedules, risks, and gains.

   ☐ Answer questions.

   ☐ Include a written document as a resource to be used during and after the meeting.

   ☐ Review implementation plan.

   ☐ Provide a detailed plan of what needs to be done, by whom, and in what sequence.

   ☐ The partnering manager is responsible for taking action.

☐ The partnering consultant conducts an evaluation according to methods established in the planning phase.

☐ The partnering manager sees that the methods are carried out during the project and after. He or she also looks at time lines to determine if goals are being met and looks at resources to determine if they are being used effectively.

☐ The manager and consultant evaluate their partnering behaviors.

Chapter
VI

MONITORING PROGRESS & OVERCOMING OBSTACLES

"To tend, unfailingly, unflinchingly, towards a goal, is the secret of success."

—Anna Pavlova

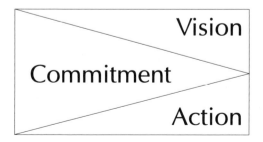

Partnering managers practice the techniques described in the preceding chapters. Although they recognize the manager-employer partnership as the primary internal alliance, managers also partner with colleagues inside and outside of the organization and with consultants when their expertise adds a needed dimension.

Partnering managers accept and recognize the challenges of partnering effectively. Effective partnering involves creating a vision of partnering, committing to partnering as a beneficial managerial approach, and putting the knowledge and techniques of partnering into action.

Through partnering, a collaborative climate is developed in which people thrive and contribute their best. Although partnering is not difficult to do, it is a skill that must be developed and used. As organizations employ partnering behaviors, problems are more effectively addressed and opportunities for growth and improvement are maximized.

To work effectively in a collaborative mode, partners must evaluate how successful they have been using the new partnering approach. The final section of this chapter contains a tool to evaluate partnering experiences.

Creating a Vision of Partnering

The partnering manager envisions successful partnerships. Knowing the value of partnering, the effective manager sees the many ways in which partnering can be implemented in the workplace and how it will benefit the individuals and the organization as a whole.

Making Commitments

Once they know the benefits of partnering, few managers would disagree with it in principle. Sound business reasons support partnering: increasing productivity, improving quality, and increasing profits. The rifts between departments, teams, and individuals can be resolved by effective partnering. Empowered to generate a win-win situation, former adversaries have successfully resolved their conflicts and increased overall performance. Committed to the improvements created through partnering, effective managers focus on their vision and on ways to implement partnering techniques.

Putting Partnering into Action

Managing the ongoing success of partnering involves the kinds of activities described in the sections that follow.

Plan Time to Partner

Most managers are inundated with too much to do, too little time to do it, and too few people to get it done. Great news would be that partnering takes little time. In reality, initiating and building partnerships requires time and effort. Once formed, however, partnerships enable managers and employees to work together more effectively—thereby saving time in the long run.

The example presented earlier in this book about designing a wellness program (Chapter IV) illustrates the result of time investment. The process took longer than hiring an outside expert to develop the program, but the benefits of building a partnership can last longer than the program that was designed. Partnering enables and encourages employees to think about the business and to develop ways to increase effectiveness. It also engenders loyalty because of the self-esteem and confidence it builds within employees.

Train Employees to Partner

To secure employees' support, the partnering manager ensures that employees receive training to develop effective partnering skills and that they feel empowered to practice those skills—knowing that their managers support and encourage partnering.

The responsibility for creating and maintaining partnerships sits with the manager. Although it is more usual for the manager to initiate partnering, an employee might also initiate partnering. For success in either case, manager-employee partnerships need a strong commitment from all parties involved.

Gain Support from Upper-Level Management

Mid-level managers and front-line supervisors can initiate partnering more effectively when bosses model the behaviors and support partnering efforts. To secure support, the partnering manager ensures that bosses are provided examples of how partnering has contributed to the organization.

Practice Partnering Techniques

Although convinced of its value, some people may not know how to partner and other people may not have received reinforcement from their managers for using partnering. Effective partnering is realized as partners move through the operating model. Based on the type of partnering one chooses to develop, the effective manager uses the appropriate procedure and process: partnering with managers (Chapter III); partnering with employees (Chapter IV); or partnering with consultants (Chapter V).

Partnerships can afford everyone the opportunity to achieve excellence. The time and resources needed to support partnering are an investment in the organization's future. By initiating the effort to establish and to nurture partnerships, managers empower themselves and their employees to build a world-class, competitive organization that no longer fears its competition.

Manage Obstacles

As effective partners move through the partnering process, they interact to enhance the outcome of their efforts. They focus on mutual problem solving and opportunity seeking. Effective partners encounter the same difficulties that any group of people who work together encounter. The value partners place on building trust and respect among one another sets them apart. Three common obstacles that partners face are managing disagreements, managing resistance to change, and managing work-style clashes.

Specific techniques for dealing with these obstacles are listed in the "Taking Action" section at the end of this chapter.

Manage Disagreements

A critical partnering skill is the ability to work through disagreements in a manner that enables all parties to win and to achieve their goals. Too often, people operate with a win-lose approach—"For me to win, you must lose"—or worse, with a lose-lose perspective—"If I lose, you can be sure that you will lose, too." Both of these attitudes are counterproductive. On the other hand, collaborators operate in a win-win mode; they work to ensure that all partners strive toward goals in such a way that everyone benefits.

However, at certain times partners interact appropriately in ways that are not collaborative; the following situations illustrate such situations:

When a decision needs to be made or an action taken immediately, partners do not have the luxury of exploring areas of agreement and disagreement. One partner alone may determine the course of action. To protect the partnership, effective partners keep one another informed of these decisions and the reasons for such unilateral action.

When one partner is concerned more about maintaining the relationship than about resolving the issue or conflict, that partner may choose to accommodate another's desires.

When no immediate action should be taken, such as when partners need time for emotions to settle or to collect more information. In some cases, time and distance help to resolve conflicts in the future.

When all parties' needs and wants cannot be met. Partners who are dealing with a highly complex situation may choose to reach a compromise in which each gives up something.

When partners disagree, they most often move to the collaborative mode, which allows partners to explore and to meet one another's needs and wants. Because all partners win in this process, they are inclined to use the process again. Collaborative behavior is the basis for effective partnering and should be the primary mode for resolving disagreement.

Manage Resistance to Change

When partners actively initiate change, they often find themselves dealing with resistance. People resist change for many reasons: they may like the status quo, or they may fear the unknown and wonder how changes will affect them. Effective partners can reduce some of the resistance by applying the following modification of the partnering model:

Create a vision of a desired future state or result.

Share the vision. Describe this future state or the end results to others so that they can see it too. Involve others as soon and as much as possible, because people are more likely to believe in what they help to create.

Gain commitment. Explain why the desired change is better than the current situation and what is in it for those affected, for the other partners, and for the organization.

Listen and respond. Provide information regarding what will and will not change, sell the benefits of the end results, acknowledge people's feelings of fear and insecurity, reinforce people as they commit to the change effort, and recognize that people process change differently.

Plan for transition. Plot a course of action to put the vision in place.

Implement the action plan. Then carry out responsibilities within the designated time line, directing others as needed.

Evaluate. Monitor progress regularly and evaluate the results of the change effort.

Manage Work-Style Clashes

Partners continually interact, as a group and in one-on-one situations. When partners work closely together, their styles can clash. To avoid this or to work through it when it happens, effective partners take the following actions:

Assess individual behavioral styles. People have a natural, preferred style of working with others. They can better understand their own styles by examining two behavioral dimensions: task/relationship and control/compliance. Understanding a person's relative focus on task versus relationship and on control versus compliance helps to create smoother interactions.

Recognize and accept one another's behavioral styles. By doing this, partners decrease the tendency to view one's own style as the only "right" way to interact with others and they learn to adjust and work with styles different from their own.

Modify styles to ease the interaction. Effective interaction requires that partners first recognize different styles; then they can learn to adjust their own behaviors to accommodate their partners' behaviors. For example, a partner who tends to dominate may need to give up some control in order to enhance the partnership. Alternatively, a partner who tends to focus mostly on facts and details may need to pursue a course of action based on someone else's instincts.

Give appropriate feedback. Partners occasionally may work with other partners who have poor interpersonal skills. This situation presents a challenge to the better-skilled partners. Given appropriate feedback, a difficult person can learn to improve his or her interpersonal skills. If no improvement is apparent, the other partners need to be patient but also to be up-front about behaviors they are willing or unwilling to tolerate. Providing feedback to the difficult person about such behaviors can reinforce effective behaviors and help to correct ineffective ones.

Evaluate Partnering Practices

Special skills are required of partners. In addition to job expertise, partners need to be able to work effectively in a collaborative mode, committed to effective interaction and goal attainment. They begin by practicing partnering behaviors and by encouraging others to do so. They must also evaluate how successful they have been in using the new partnering techniques. A tool to help individuals evaluate their partnering experiences is provided at the end of this chapter.

Summary

Dynamic partnerships evolve when partners share mutual goals, needs, and interests. By working together, dynamic partners create win-win situations. Today's competitive global environment requires people within organizations to form alliances, to share a vision, and to work together to reach that vision.

Dynamic partners are committed to specific goals, enabling them to identify roles, to set time frames, and to select methods for achieving goals. Managers partner with other managers and with employees. These partnerships may seek the support of other partners—internal or external consultants.

The goal of partnering is to identify each partner's skills and empower him or her to use those skills. Partners therefore work together collaboratively. They communicate the desire for a win-win situation for all partners and for the organization. This challenges them to share information, resources, and responsibilities. From the time that partners determine their willingness to work together through to the point at which they evaluate their achievements, partners strive to maintain trust and respect for one another's talents. This contributes to higher productivity, improved products and services, and a better quality of work life.

To employ effective partnering practices, one must do the following:

☐ Create a vision of successful partnering.

☐ Make the commitment to partner.

☐ Put partnering into action.

    ☐ Plan time to partner.

    ☐ Train employees to partner.

    ☐ Gain support from superiors for partnering.

    ☐ Practice partnering techniques using the appropriate procedure and process found in the following chapters:

    Chapter III: Partnering with Managers

    Chapter IV: Partnering with Employees

    Chapter V: Partnering with Consultants

☐ Learn to manage disagreements.

    ☐ Identify and respect partners' wants and needs.

    ☐ Clarify partners' main concerns.

    ☐ Share own wants, needs, and concerns with partners.

    ☐ Determine compatibilities and differences.

    ☐ Conduct a two-way communication with partners to clarify the preceding points.

    ☐ Design a collaborative plan of action that does not compromise either partner's position.

    ☐ Identify options that enable partners to reach an acceptable solution even if goals are not compatible.

☐ Learn to manage resistance to change.

    ☐ Have a vision of a desired future state or result.

    ☐ Share the vision.

☐   Gain commitment.

☐   Listen and respond.

☐   Plan for transition.

☐   Implement the action plan.

☐   Monitor progress and evaluate change-effort results.

☐ Learn to manage work-style clashes.

☐   Assess individual behavioral styles.

☐   Recognize and accept one another's behavioral styles.

☐   Modify style to aid the interaction.

☐   Provide feedback to people about behaviors to reinforce effective behaviors and to help correct ineffective ones.

☐ Evaluate partnering practices according to the list that follows.

HOW WELL DID WE PARTNER?

Instructions: Evaluate your partnering practices by answering "yes," "somewhat," or "no" to each of the following questions.

Part One: Use of the Operating Model

Vision

_____   1. We shared a clear vision of what we wanted to accomplish.

_____   2. We understood how our work fits into the big picture.

Commitment

_____   3. We shared a commitment to our goals.

_____   4. We believed in making a difference with our product/service.

Action

Planning

_____ 5. We set clear goals for the partnership.

_____ 6. We defined our roles and responsibilities.

_____ 7. We established time lines.

_____ 8. We determined diagnostic methods to use.

_____ 9. We communicated throughout the process.

_____ 10. We determined the resources needed.

_____ 11. We defined the evaluation process.

_____ 12. We specified our agreements in writing.

Diagnosing

_____ 13. We used a variety of diagnostic techniques.

_____ 14. We collected and analyzed the data.

Making Decisions

_____ 15. We summarized the information gathered in diagnosis.

_____ 16. We determined various courses of action.

_____ 17. We provided written documentation of the recommendations.

Implementing

_____ 18. We outlined specific plans and time lines for all involved.

_____ 19. We established checkpoints to monitor our progress.

Evaluating

_____ 20. We evaluated the results we achieved.

_____ 21. We determined a plan for improvement.

Part Two: Use of Partnering Behaviors

_____ 22. We assessed our willingness to partner.

_____ 23. We were honest about our strengths and weak-nesses and interacted effectively with one another.

_____ 24. We discussed our preferred working styles.

_____ 25. We chose partners who possessed knowledge, talents, and resources.

_____ 26. We involved others in the change process.

_____ 27. We created an environment of openness and trust for all involved.

_____ 28. We challenged one another.

_____ 29. We took necessary risks.

_____ 30. We shared information, skills, authority, and resources.

_____ 31. We found opportunities and empowered others.

_____ 32. We solved problems creatively and sought opportunities and encouraged others to do so.

_____ 33. We managed difficult people appropriately.

_____ 34. We listened actively to one another's view points.

_____ 35. We managed disagreements appropriately.

_____ 36. We kept one another informed throughout.

_____ 37. We mutually agreed to any changes that needed to be made.

_____ 38. We gave one another performance feedback.

_____ 39. We fulfilled all agreed-on responsibilities.

_____ 40. We evaluated the partnering relationship throughout the process.

_____ 41. We recognized and celebrated our successes.

Use of Partnering and the Partnering Model

Based on an assessment of your current partnering practices, consider what changes would improve your partnering. Acknowledge your achievements to reinforce your success and momentum. Develop action statements to focus more effectively on developing strong partnerships. Finally, schedule the action items to put them in motion.

1. What I am doing well in practicing partnering? What are my greatest strengths?

2. Where would I choose to make modifications and/or improvements?

3. What I am doing well in developing partnerships? What are my greatest strengths?

4. Where would I choose to make modifications and/or improvements?